REVISED EDITION

MESSIAH
in
THE FEASTS
of
ISRAEL

SAM NADLER

WORD OF MESSIAH MINI
CHARLOTTE, NC

D1161006

TABLE OF CONTENTS

PROLOGUE

Appointments with a Purpose

Across the ages, God has sought after the people of Israel, in order to bless them and make them a blessing to many peoples (Genesis 12:2-3). He also gave Israel a sacred trust— to bear His Name and to be the nation from which His redemptive plan for the world would go forth (John 4:22). This plan is illustrated in the various feasts He ordained. These feasts are called *moedim* in Hebrew, meaning "appointments" (Leviticus 23:2). In a sense, these times constitute God's agenda with His redeemed people. Ultimately, they provide a Biblical and historical foundation for faith in Yeshua.[1]

I wrote this book to present my Saviour in context. Messiah was to be the fulfillment of the Feasts; He is the purpose for their existence. Indeed, all of the Scriptures are fulfilled in Messiah Yeshua, just as "with regard to a festival... or a Sabbath day— these are a shadow of the things to come, but the substance belongs to Messiah" (Colossians 2:16-17).

Even as all Scripture is inspired and profitable, these "shadows" are relevant for followers of Messiah today, because they never stop pointing to Him (1 Timothy 3:16). I hope that by reading this book you will have a clearer picture of the amazing, incomprehensible love of God, and be motivated to walk closer with Yeshua. They really do speak of Him!

---

[1] Yeshua is Jesus' name in Hebrew. There is a glossary of Jewish and Messianic terminology on page 234

The seven annual appointed times found in Leviticus 23 will take up the majority of our attention. The calendar as it is laid out there begins to unfold in springtime. The first three times— Passover, Unleavened Bread[2], and Firstfruits— illustrate the redemption accomplished in Yeshua's first coming. The fourth, Pentecost, speaks of "the Body of Messiah" being established in the earth. In the fall, at the seventh month of the biblical year, we observe Trumpets, the Day of Atonement, and Booths. These focus our attention on the period of time yet to come, the consummation of God's redemptive program.

The material involves texts, but also ancient and contemporary traditions and different layers of meaning. At times it can seem overwhelming, especially when it is all new for the reader. We've placed a chart in the back (pp 228-229) for you to keep track of the larger themes as you progress through the material.

Also, there are additional feasts celebrated today that do not appear in Leviticus 23. We will look at two: Hanukkah and Purim. Though established later than the seven above, they nonetheless have unusual significance for followers of Messiah.

We begin with the Sabbath, which is celebrated weekly and not annually. Sabbath-rest is really the theme and goal of God's plan. Let's dive in and take a look at these great gatherings of God!

---

[2] Passover and Unleavened Bread are considered together in chapter 2, since they are observed at the same time.

GOD IS RELATING
TO HIS PEOPLE

through

SHABBAT

CHAPTER 1

SABBATH

THE THEME OF
GOD'S REDEMPTION PROGRAM

IN THE TORAH

> ...on the seventh day God finished his work that He had done, and He rested on the seventh day from all His work that he had done. (Genesis 2:2)

> The LORD spoke again to Moses, saying, "Speak to the sons of Israel, and say to them, 'The LORD's appointed times which you shall proclaim as holy convocations– My appointed times are these: For six days work may be done; but on the seventh day there is a sabbath of complete rest, a holy convocation. You shall not do any work; it is a sabbath to the LORD in all your dwellings.'" (Leviticus 23:1-3)

Leviticus 23 is God's appointment schedule to meet with His redeemed people. The weekly Sabbath, or *Shabbat* in Hebrew, points to the theme and goal of God's redemption program.

This day was established before the giving of the Law. After creation God ceased from His labors and rested on the Sabbath (Genesis 2:1-3). The root word in Hebrew for Shabbat is *yashav*, meaning to rest, or to sit down. Yet it was not as though He said, "I will take a little break and get back to work first thing next week." No, His work was done; it was to be Sabbath-rest from that point onward. However, through disobedience to God, man lost his true rest in Him.

UNDERSTANDING SHABBAT

Knowing these things from the beginning, the goal of God's work was to restore true Sabbath rest, which comes ultimately through Messiah. How do we find rest, peace, and a dynamic relationship with God in our lives? We find some clues in the study of Sabbath itself.

One cannot restore Shabbat if one does not know what it was intended to be, according to the Scriptures. Without this understanding of Shabbat, we may assume certain traditional issues that are not true at all. Some think it is an optional day off. Others think that Sunday is the new Christian or replacement Sabbath. Also there are those who think it is to be kept simply as an obligation in the Law. Of course, if that is so, then we must work not just five, but six days a week. After all, the commandment says, "Six days shall you labor, and do all your work" (Exodus 20:6). That means no two-day weekends! What, then, is Sabbath really about?

SHABBAT IS ABOUT RELATIONSHIP

In a sense, when God finished creating the world He then created rest. In fact, it may help to know that the word "Shabbat" is related to the word *shevet*– to dwell and abide. The Scripture describes it as a time when God would enjoy and actually dwell with His creation.

> They heard the sound of the LORD God walking in the garden in the cool of the day... Then the LORD God called to the man, and said to him, "Where are you?" (Genesis 3:8-9)

God desired fellowship with Adam and Eve. On the Sabbath, God made the world His dwelling place, His resting place; it was a time to fellowship with His creation. So in Genesis 2:3, God declared the Sabbath holy and blessed, for in it God wants to relate to you.

We all use different times to strengthen our relationships. For example, we celebrate wedding anniversaries to remember, renew, and strengthen our marriage vows. Every time you do something special– go out to eat, buy a gift– you are reliving and renewing your marriage vow and strengthening your marriage bond. For followers of Messiah in their relationship with God, the Lord's Supper (*Zikkaron*) and believer's immersion (*Mikveh*) work like this. They strengthen our relationship with the Lord by illustrating what He has done for us.

This then is the essence of Shabbat. God desires relationship with His creation, and a weekly time of rest was set aside for that purpose.

CREATION AND REDEMPTION

Shabbat pictures God's goal: that by *His works* we would dwell with Him and relate to Him. We read in Exodus 20:10, "the seventh day is a Sabbath *to* the LORD your God" *(Shabbat l'Adonai Elohechah)*. Thus, Shabbat is not just a day off from work, but also a day to the Lord, a time to relate to God. How do we relate to God through Shabbat? There are two ways.

First of all, as His creation: "For in six days the LORD made the heavens and the earth, the sea and all that is in them" (Exodus 20:11). Of all His creation, God created only people in His own image (Genesis 1:26-28). He did this so we could both relate to Him and represent Him in the world. He created us to think and feel, so we could choose to have faith in Him and follow Him.

Secondly, as His redeemed: "God said to Israel, 'Remember you were slaves in Egypt. The Lord brought you out with a mighty hand and an outstretched arm. Therefore, the Lord your God commands you to observe the Sabbath day'" (Deuteronomy 5:15). God redeemed us for Himself. He delivered us from bondage and judgment not merely to escape punishment, but that we might be His people and relate to Him.

These are the two aspects signified by the Sabbath– creation and redemption. In fact, following creation, the next work that God performed was a sacrifice; the bloody death of an animal was needed to cover the sin of Adam and Eve (Genesis 3:21). God's work of creation may have been over by the seventh day, but because of sin, God's work was to redeem His lost creation.

This work of redemption was ultimately accomplished through the death of Messiah where Yeshua declared, "It is finished" (John 19:30). When we find rest in Messiah, then we can relate to God and enjoy His peace and harmony, just as Shabbat pictures. This explains why the concept of peace is so important on Shabbat. One of the most common traditional Sabbath greetings is *Shabbat Shalom*, which means "Sabbath peace." The main idea of the Sabbath is peace: not just peace between man and his neighbor, but peace between man and His Creator. This is the very peace that Yeshua brings. As the Prince of Peace, Messiah has the sole authority to grant peace. There can be no true peace, with God or with man, apart from Him.

GOD'S REMINDER TO REST

Why can't people find rest? Because apart from God, we sense the personal inadequacy of our lives, which is a by-product of sin. Sin alienates us from God. We fall short and we do not measure up. As a result we feel that we must somehow do more, have more, and accomplish more before we can feel secure and satisfied. We might think, "My house, my career, and my family are my life, and until it measures up I haven't made it." While these endeavors may be worthwhile, they are not what our lives were meant to be about. Apart from God we create our own gods, in our own image, to make us feel secure and worthwhile.

These gods could never and will never save or secure us. Our own works cannot enable us to truly measure up. Yet that is the point. We do not rest in our finished works, but in His finished work.

Each Shabbat, if at no other time, we must realize our own rest is in the Lord. We can relate to Him because of His finished work of creation and redemption. Apart from God's redemption, no one can relate to Him. For believers, once each week through Shabbat, we strengthen and renew our faith in our relationship with God.

A SANCTIFYING SIGN

> But as for you, speak to the sons of Israel, saying, "You shall surely observe My Sabbaths; for this is a sign between Me and you throughout your generations, that you may know that I am the LORD who sanctifies you." (Exodus 31:13)

A wedding ring is a reminder of a present and sanctifying (set apart) relationship. It reminds you that you are "set apart" to your spouse. Just like that wedding ring, the sign of Shabbat is a reminder of the sanctifying relationship between God and Israel. A relationship that sanctifies, that is holy (*kadosh* in Hebrew), sets us apart unto God for His purpose and glory.

Are you set apart unto God? By definition the word "saints" means "set apart ones." All believers are set apart. Therefore, in light of who we are in Messiah, we are to be setting our lives apart unto God. To the degree you set your life apart to God, to that degree you demonstrate that you value your relationship with the Lord. Do you have a Shabbat? Do you take time each week to reorient your life and set it apart unto God?

Shabbat is a re-prioritizing of a relationship with God in your life. Since relationships take time to develop, we need to spend time developing our relationship with the Lord. Shabbat is the sign of a life relating to God.

A SIGN OF ETERNITY

Shabbat is not only a reminder of peace we have by faith in Messiah right now, but a *sign* of future and perfect rest yet to come!

> It [Shabbat] is an eternal sign between Me and the sons of Israel; for in six days the LORD made heaven and earth, but on the seventh day He ceased from labor, and was refreshed. (Exodus 31:17)

The Scriptures calls Shabbat "an eternal sign" or "sign forever." Literally in Hebrew the phrase *ot hu l'olam* means "it is a sign *to* eternity," or a "sign for eternity." Have you ever been driving on your way to New York City and seen signs pointing to NYC? You did not stop the car at the sign, get out and say, "We're here!" No, the sign lets you know that there is a New York City, a destination yet to come. In a similar way, Shabbat illustrates and gives a glimpse of eternity, our eternal rest in the Lord. Shabbat pictures God's rest, His own unchanging serenity that He has in Himself. It is a rest that the day itself cannot provide, but can only be found in Him. This is a rest that God calls "My Rest" (Psalm 95:11; Hebrews 4:3).

Thus the Sabbath became a picture of a day where God's rest will be truly experienced forever by His redeemed creation. Also the rabbis wrote:

> What is a foretaste of the world to come? The Sabbath. (Bereshit Rabbah 17:7)

> This world is like the eve of the Sabbath, and the next world is like the Sabbath. If one does not prepare, of what shall he partake? (Ruth Rabbah 3:3)

14

The Messianic Age is also called *yom shekulo shabbat*, or the day when all is Sabbath: "for the day (i.e., the world to come) will be all Sabbath and rest for everlasting life" (Mishnah Tamid 7:4, 33b).

As the prophets promised, the Messianic Age will be a time when "every man will sit under his vine and beneath his fig tree, and none will make them afraid" (Micah 4:4). Under Messiah's reign finally there will be the peace and Shabbat rest that all mankind has long desired. Shabbat was meant to be a picture of the eternal rest we have in the Messiah.

SHABBAT IS REALIZED IN THE MESSIAH

Yeshua said, "Come to Me, all you who are weary and heavy-laden, and I will give you rest. Learn from Me... and you will find rest for your souls" (Matthew 11:28-19). Messiah is the reality that Shabbat promises. He is our Shabbat peace. "Therefore, having been justified by faith, we have peace with God through our Lord Messiah Yeshua" (Romans 5:1). This fulfillment has come in Yeshua. He is the fulfillment of all that Shabbat pictures.

This is why, out of the Ten Commandments, the Shabbat commandment is the only one *not* reiterated in the New Covenant. Shabbat is a type of Messiah; a foreshadowing of the true rest that comes only in Him (Colossians 2:16-17).

The New Covenant does not give rules and regulations for a particular day for worship, though early believers in Yeshua (first through the third centuries) generally worshipped on Shabbat. The Counsel of Laodicea (AD 336) sought to transfer the day from Saturday to Sunday.

In fact, when the Bishop of Rome insisted on Sunday as a replacement, worship on Shabbat was commonplace elsewhere. Ambrose, the renowned bishop of Milan, Italy, said that when he was in Milan he observed Saturday, but when in Rome he observed Sunday. This gave rise to the proverb, "when in Rome, do as the Romans do."[3]

Along with Ambrose, we understand that the Sabbath day has never been changed to Sunday. However, I do respect his flexibility, and believe God desires our fellowship every day. The real thing to consider then is: what is the true motivation for Shabbat?

We will look at the Spring Feasts starting with Passover in the next chapter, but let's skip ahead a little. Why would someone "keep the feast," celebrating Passover as Paul says (1 Corinthians 5:8)? Is it merely to speak of the past events in Egypt? No, it is because "Messiah our Passover has come"; we celebrate and proclaim the full redemption from sin which was typified by the redemption from Egypt.

Likewise, why do we worship on Shabbat? Is it only to have a day of remembering creation and redemption from Egypt? No, while those aspects never get cancelled out, there is much more. We worship on Shabbat to proclaim the full redemption and rest that the day itself only typifies. Yeshua Himself is our eternal rest and redemption.

Thus, every Shabbat, Messianic congregations gather to recognize the redemption and new creation in Yeshua, our true Sabbath. The real issue, then, is not merely being faithful to a day, but this: are you redeemed by, relating to, and resting in the Lord?

3 cited in Heylyn, "History of the Sabbath," Part 2, par. 5, pp73-74. London: 1636.

So there remains a Sabbath rest for the people of God. For the one who has entered His rest has himself also rested from his works, as God did from His. (Hebrews 4:9-10)

As Shabbat instructs us to rest from our labors, more importantly it focuses us to rest in the Lord. Shabbat not only reminds us of what we are living for, but whom we are to be living with forever! Let us take time to develop our relationship of rest in Messiah.

QUESTIONS FOR SHABBAT:

1. What is the Hebrew word for Sabbath and what does it mean? *rest ,*

2. What were the two aspects of the Sabbath found in the Hebrew Scriptures? *creation , redemption*

3. How do you relate to God through the Sabbath?

4. How does the Sabbath picture eternity? *future of perfect rest*

5. Why is there no commandment regarding Sabbath in the New Covenant Scriptures?
the Messiah

GOD IS REDEEMING
HIS PEOPLE

through

PESACH

CHAPTER 2

THE FEAST OF PASSOVER

MESSIAH OUR PASSOVER LAMB

IN THE TORAH

Now the LORD said to Moses and Aaron in the land of Egypt, "This month shall be the beginning of months for you; it is to be the first month of the year to you. Speak to all the congregation of Israel, saying, 'On the tenth of this month they are each one to take a lamb for themselves, according to their fathers' households, a lamb for each household. Now if the household is too small for a lamb, then he and his neighbor nearest to his house are to take one according to the number of persons in them; according to what each man should eat, you are to divide the lamb. Your lamb shall be an unblemished male a year old; you may take it from the sheep or from the goats. And you shall keep it until the fourteenth day of the same month, then the whole assembly of the congregation of Israel is to kill it at twilight. Moreover, they shall take some of the blood and put it on the two doorposts and on the lintel of the houses in which they eat it. ... Now you shall eat it in this manner: with your loins girded, your sandals on your feet, and your staff in your hand; and you shall eat it in haste– it is the LORD's Passover. For I will go through the land of Egypt on that night, and will strike down all the first-born in the land of Egypt, both man and beast; and against all the gods of Egypt I will execute judgments– I am the LORD. And the blood shall be a sign for you on the houses where you live; and when I see the blood I will pass over you, and no plague will befall you to destroy you when I strike the land of Egypt.'" (Exodus 12:1-7, 11-13)

"In the first month, on the fourteenth day of the month at twilight is the LORD's Passover. Then on the fifteenth day of the same month there is the Feast of Unleavened Bread to the LORD; for seven days you shall eat unleavened bread. On the first day you shall have a holy convocation; you shall not do any laborious work. But for seven days you shall present an offering by fire to the LORD. On the seventh day is a holy convocation; you shall not do any laborious work." (Leviticus 23:5-8)

I remember from my childhood in New York City, when the family celebrated Passover every year. We would all crowd into our small apartment where my grandfather would lead our *seder*.[1] The fragrance of beef and chicken wafted through the air, the family squeezed in around the table, and grandpa donned a kittel, the white ceremonial robe worn by the leader. It was always a joyous occasion.

Passover (*pesach*) is an eight day festival kept in remembrance of the Lord's "passing over" the houses of the Israelites, when the first born of all the Egyptians

---

[1] A *seder* literally means "order," referring to the ancient service and meal held usually on the first night of Passover. This chapter will utilize the seder to explore the Messianic meaning of Passover.

were slain. It came to be identified with the "Feast of Unleavened Bread" (Exodus 23:15, Leviticus 23:6), because during this time no leavened bread is eaten or kept in the household. Traditionally, Jewish people understand this deliverance from bondage as a time to reflect upon and appreciate our personal and political freedom. During the meal we read from a Haggadah, a booklet that leads families through the Exodus story.[2]

This feast is probably the most well known of all the Biblical feasts. Many of us may know it from Cecil B. DeMille's film, *The Ten Commandments*, which is the Exodus story plus a few Hollywood liberties. However, despite its familiarity, there is a powerful concept at the center of this feast that is often overlooked: personal deliverance through the blood of the Lamb.

To better understand the Feast of Passover let us first take a look at the background of the story. Four hundred years prior to the days of Moses, there was a famine in the land of Canaan. This famine caused the Patriarch Jacob (Israel) to travel south to Egypt where his favorite, long lost son, Joseph, turned up as Vice-Pharaoh, and became quite a hero (Genesis 37-47).

Time passed and as the Scriptures record, "Joseph died, and all his brothers and all that generation. But the sons of Israel were fruitful and increased greatly, and multiplied, and became exceedingly mighty, so that the land was filled with them" (Exodus 1:6-7). Eventually, "a new king arose over Egypt, who did not know Joseph" (Exodus 1:8).

---

[2] For an example, see *The Messianic Passover Haggadah* from Word of Messiah Ministries

Feeling threatened by the increase of the number of Hebrews in Goshen, Pharaoh sought a way to deal with his perceived problem:

> "Come, let us deal wisely with them, lest they multiply and in the event of war, they also join themselves to those who hate us, and fight against us, and depart from the land." So they appointed taskmasters over them to afflict them with hard labor. And they built for Pharaoh storage cities, Pithom and Raamses. But the more they afflicted them, the more they multiplied and the more they spread out, so that they were in dread of the sons of Israel. (Exodus 1:10-12)

Seeing his plan was having little effect, Pharaoh enacted a most heartless policy against the Israelites:

> And he [Pharaoh] said, "When you are helping the Hebrew women to give birth and see them upon the birthstool, if it is a son, then you shall put him to death; but if it is a daughter, then she shall live." (Exodus 1:16)

Moses grew up and was educated in Pharaoh's household during this time. He later had to flee Egypt and spent forty years on the backside of the desert where, unbeknownst to him, God was preparing Moses to return to Egypt, confront Pharaoh, and demand he let God's people go. After a series of nine horrendous plagues, Pharaoh was still unwilling to comply with God's will. The tenth and final plague would be the straw that broke the camel's back, so to speak. God would destroy every firstborn in Egypt, unless the blood of a lamb was applied to the doorposts of each home. Hebrews and Egyptians alike would be spared this judgment upon the gods of Egypt, but only when God saw the blood on the door.

> The blood shall be a sign for you on the houses where you are. And when I see the blood, I will pass over you; and the plague shall not be on you to destroy you when I strike the land of Egypt. (Exodus 12:13)

This issue of redemption may become more clear as we consider the contemporary celebration, which draws from traditions in use even in Yeshua's day. In many Passover *seders*, Israel's past deliverance is emphasized without much present relevance. However in a Messianic Passover *seder*, we emphasize that God accomplished our past redemption in order to give hope for the future, specifically as it pertains to the Messiah and His deliverance. Historically, this significance came to light at Yeshua's final *seder* with His disciples before His death:

> Then came the Day of Unleavened Bread, when the Passover must be killed. And He [Yeshua] sent Peter and John saying, "Go and prepare the Passover for us, that we may eat."
>
> So they said to Him, "Where do You want us to prepare?"
>
> And He replied to them, "Behold, when you have entered the city, a man will meet you carrying a pitcher of water; follow him into the house that he enters. Then you shall say to the master of the house, 'The Teacher says to you, "Where is the guest room where I may eat the Passover with My disciples?"' Then he will show you a large, furnished upper room; there make ready." So they went and found it just as He had said to them, and they prepared the Passover. (Luke 22:7-13)

CELEBRATING THE PASSOVER SEDER

As the passage states, when Messiah Yeshua celebrated the Passover just before His sacrificial death for our atonement, He sent two followers to prepare the room for the *seder*. These preparations focus on the removal of all leavened foods (made with yeast, or *chametz*) from the home. During the eight days of Passover, only foods that have no yeast are eaten. The most well known unleavened food is the bread, *matzah*. There are two reasons why only unleavened bread is eaten during Passover:

The historical reason: Thirty-four hundred years ago, when the Jewish people were about to be delivered by God's mighty arm from bondage in Egypt, God told them to be ready to move on a moment's notice. That's why historically we eat only matzah at Passover. It is sometimes called "the bread of haste," because God said to Israel "you came out of the land of Egypt in haste" (Deuteronomy 16:3).

The spiritual reason: Unleavened bread is made without yeast. Even as leaven or yeast puffs up the bread to make it seem greater than it is, so also the Scripture consistently uses leaven as a picture of pride, sin, and unbelief. This is why yeast was not permitted as part of the normal meal offerings in the Tabernacle (Leviticus 2:11). Thus, Messiah warns His followers regarding false teachers, "Watch out and beware of the leaven of the Pharisees and the Sadducees" (Matthew 16:6).

Today, in homes where Passover is observed, celebration generally begins after leavened products are removed. The head of the house searches for any crumb of leaven in order to purge his home of defilement.

25

Traditionally, the father would use a feather and a spoon to sweep up any last bit of chametz, even as over the years Jewish tradition produced many folios of legal guidelines focused on the stringent removal of leaven from homes.[3]

Yet, for believers, the preparations are not just for the home. Rather, the home reflects the heart. Paul used this idea to correct the prideful Corinthian believers:

> Your boasting is not good. Do you not know that a little leaven leavens the whole lump of dough? Clean out the old leaven so that you may be a new lump, just as you are in fact unleavened. For Messiah our Passover also has been sacrificed. Therefore let us celebrate the feast, not with old leaven, nor with the leaven of malice and wickedness, but with the unleavened bread of sincerity and truth. (1 Corinthians 5:6-8)

Paul refers to the tradition of cleansing the home to illustrate the need for the cleansing of our hearts. The old leaven refers not to Jewish traditions as some have erroneously thought, but to unconfessed sin in the soul. Yeshua knew, as Paul learned, that without proper preparation there could not be full participation in Passover's spiritual blessings. Why do more believers in Messiah not enjoy the new life He brings? Believers today, like the first century Corinthians, need to "clean out the old leaven," the unconfessed sin that hinders intimacy with the Lord.

Where there is unconfessed sin, there are obstacles in relating to God (Isaiah 59:2). We are saved because of His once-and-for-all atonement for sins (Hebrews 10:12), but in our messy lives we often do not know the joy of that

---

[3] Pesahim 1a-93b

salvation, a joy which only comes from a close walk with God (1 John 1:7). So we confess our sins to the Lord and thank Him for the full fellowship we have in Messiah (1 John 1:9).

So as Yeshua and His disciples approached Jerusalem, the Scripture records that "they prepared the Passover. When the hour had come, He reclined at the table, and the apostles with Him" (Luke 22:13-14). "The hour" spoken of here would be at sunset, when the new day begins according to the Biblical calendar. Yeshua and His disciples reclined at the table, as was the custom in those days. The guests would be eating at very low tables. A person would lie on his left side at an angle, extend his feet out from the table, and usually eat with his right hand. The person next to him would 'recline' with their head somewhat close to his neighbor's chest, and so on around the table.

In a seder today, after the home is cleansed and the heart is prepared, the woman of the house begins the evening by lighting the candles and reciting a Hebrew blessing over them:

> Blessed are you O Lord our God, King of the universe Who has sanctified us through faith in Yeshua the Messiah the Light of the world and in His Name we kindle the Passover Lights.[4]

With the candles lit, the head of the house makes sure each person has a cup of the "fruit of the vine." The Seder is divided into four sections, and we drink four times from the cup to remember the blessings of redemption in Exodus 6:6-7:

---

[4] This is a Messianic version of the blessing.

1. *The Cup of Sanctification* remembers, "I will bring you out from under the burdens of the Egyptians."

2. *The Cup of Plagues* remembers, *"I* will deliver you from their bondage."

3. *The Cup of Redemption* remembers, "I will also redeem you with an outstretched arm and with great judgments."

4. *The Cup of Praise* remembers, "I will take you for My people."

THE MIDDLE PIECE

After the first blessing over the cup, tradition has the person leading the *seder* ceremonial hand-washing which is called *urchatz*. However, it was at this point in the *seder* that Yeshua, rather than washing His own hands, girded Himself with a towel, "poured water into a basin and began to wash the disciples' feet, and to wipe them with the towel with which He was girded" (John 13:5). Messiah's humility no doubt stunned His disciples, as He demonstrated servant leadership in this act. It also sheds new light on the Scriptures:

> Who is like the LORD our God, Who dwells on high,
> Who humbles Himself to behold the things that are in
> the heavens and in the earth? (Psalm 113:5-6)

Next, we pass around the parsley, or *karpas* in Hebrew, which is the first of the "bitter herbs." Each person dips his sprig of parsley into salt water and after the traditional Hebrew prayer is chanted, it is eaten together. The green parsley, by its color, illustrates our lives, and the salt water, our tears. In bondage our lives were drenched in grief and tears. Messiah came to bear our sorrows from sin, and just as God delivered the Jewish people through the salty Red Sea, He also wipes away every bitter tear. As Isaiah wrote:

> He is despised and rejected by men, a man of sorrows and acquainted with grief... Surely He has borne our griefs and carried our sorrows. (Isaiah 53:3-4)

The highlight during this first cup section is the removal of what is called the *Afikomen*. On the Passover table there is a *matzah tash* (bread bag) containing three slices of *matzah*. This bag of *matzah* is also called the *Echad,* or unity.

As a child, this was always a mystery to me. When we would celebrate Passover together around the table, I would wonder, "Why three pieces of *matzah*? How about two or maybe four?"

Yet three it was. And different years, I would learn new traditions as to why three were inside the one. One year, I was taught that the Unity represented the Patriarchs: Abraham, Isaac, and Jacob. As the second or middle Patriarch, Isaac, alone was taken out in Genesis 22 to be sacrificed, so also the middle slice of *matzah* alone was taken out at this time. Another year I was taught that the Unity (*Echad*) represented the people of Israel, the priesthood (*cohenim*), and the Lord. As the middle section alone the priesthood made sacrifices to reconcile God and man, so also the middle slice of *matzah* alone was taken out and broken.

At this point in the *seder*, the head of the house removes the middle piece of *matzah*, breaks it in half, wraps one half in a white linen cloth and hides it. This hidden piece of *matzah* becomes the *Afikomen*, which stays hidden until a child finds it during the third cup section.

Afikomen is a Greek verb meaning "that which comes after." It is generally referred to as dessert because it is the last item eaten in the meal. We shall return to this mysterious and ancient symbol at the third cup, when the children are encouraged to find the hidden *Afikomen*, and the child who finds it receives a reward from the head of the house.

BITTERNESS OF BONDAGE AND BETRAYAL

As the Seder progresses through the second cup section, the concepts of bondage and deliverance are brought into even clearer focus. The second cup is blessed and everyone partakes together. Then the head of the house takes another piece of *matzah*, holds it up and says, "This is the bread of our affliction."

The *matzah* presents a vivid picture of Messiah's body. Both pierced through with holes and striped by the baking process, the look of *matzah* gives an illustration of Messiah's suffering prophesied in Isaiah 53:5, "For He was pierced through for our transgressions and with His stripes we are healed."

The *matzah* is passed around and each person breaks off a piece. Together we recite the traditional blessing before eating it:

Baruch Atah Adonai Eloheinu Melech ha Olam,
Ha-motzti lechem min ha'aretz.

Blessed are you O Lord our God King of the Universe,
Who brings forth bread from the ground.

Next there is a second partaking of the bitter herbs. This time it is the horseradish or *maror* in Hebrew. The head of the house takes a piece of *matzah* and dips it into the *maror* making sure he puts enough on to bring a tear to his eye when he eats it. He then passes it around the table so each person can put *maror* on a piece of *matzah* (Exodus 12:8).

It is possibly at this point that Yeshua indicated the impending betrayal by one of His own disciples, "Behold, the hand of him that betrays me is with me on the table. And truly the Son of man goes, as it was determined: but woe unto that man by whom he is betrayed" (Luke 22:21, 22). John's account gives us more detail:

> Then the disciples looked at one another, perplexed about whom He spoke. Now there was leaning on Yeshua's bosom one of His disciples, whom Jesus loved. Simon Peter therefore motioned to him to ask who it was of whom He spoke. Then, leaning back on Yeshua's breast, he said to Him, "Lord, who is it?" Yeshua answered, "It is he to whom I shall give a piece of bread when I have dipped it." And having dipped the bread, He gave it to Judas Iscariot, the son of Simon. (John 13:22-26)

This was the fulfillment of David's prophecy from Psalm 41:9, "Even my close friend in whom I trusted, Who ate my bread, has lifted up his heel against me" (Zechariah 11:12-13; Matthew 26:15, 27:3-9).

Though the bitterness of the bondage of sin is echoed by the prophets down through the ages, the goodness of God is magnified in His gracious redemption of the sinner who repents:

I will pour upon the house of David, and upon the inhabitants of Jerusalem, the Spirit of grace and of supplications. And they shall look upon Me whom they have pierced, and they shall mourn for Him, as one mourns for his only son, and shall be in bitterness for Him, as one that is in bitterness for his firstborn. (Zechariah 12:10)

Indeed it was for my own peace that I had great bitterness; and You have lovingly delivered my soul from the pit of corruption, for You have cast all my sins behind Your back. (Isaiah 38:17)

THE SWEETNESS IN OUR LABOR

Made with chopped apples and spices, *charoseth* symbolizes the mortar and labor used to make bricks for Pharoah. The head of the house puts *charoseth* on a piece of *matzah* then passes the *charoseth* for all to take and eat (with bitter herbs, optional). The sweet food reminds us that our labor seems sweet, knowing our redemption draws near. Regardless of our bitter difficulties, troubles and trials, those who know the Redeemer, Yeshua, have two promises from God:

✡ *The promise of His Presence*: "He has said, 'I will never leave you nor forsake you'." (Hebrews 13:5; Joshua 1:5)

✡ *The promise of His Purpose*: "We know that all things work together for good to them that love God, to them who are the called according to his purpose." (Romans 8:28)

The *haggigah*, or egg, reminds us of the temple and the holy day temple sacrifices which are no more. The egg is round and endless, like life eternal. Coming out of bondage is like being brought back from the dead.

Similarly, for our redemption Messiah was raised from the dead. Yeshua said, "I am the resurrection and the life. He who believes in Me, though he may die, he shall live" (John 11:29). The redeemed of the Lord shall be with Messiah forever. We have been released from our bondage in sin and the fear of death. Hallelujah!

THE FOUR QUESTIONS

At this point, a child (under thirteen years of age) traditionally asks 'the four questions.' These four are summarized by one question, "Why is this night different from all other nights?"

1. "On all other nights we eat either leavened or unleavened bread; why on this night do we eat *Matzah*, unleavened bread?"

2. "On all other nights we eat vegetables of all kinds; why on this night do we eat bitter herbs?"

3. "On all other nights we do not dip at all; why on this night do we dip twice?"

4. "On all other nights we sit upright or reclining; why on this night do we all recline?"

These four questions allow the children to get involved in the *seder*, and in response the head of the house tells the Passover story from Exodus 1-12. God saw Israel in Egyptian bondage and sent Moses to demand from Pharaoh the release of the Jewish people. Pharaoh refused, so God sent a series of ten judgments upon Egypt: Blood, Frogs, Vermin, Flies, Pestilence, Boils, Hail, Locusts, Darkness, and Slaying of the Firstborn.

The culmination of these was a horrible affliction indeed. Why such a horrific plague? Scripture teaches that what had been done to Israel, God's firstborn of the nations, would be done to their firstborn.

> Then you shall say to Pharaoh, "Thus says the LORD: 'Israel is My son, My firstborn. So I say to you, let My son go that he may serve Me. But if you refuse to let him go, indeed I will kill your son, your firstborn.'" (Exodus 4:22-23)

The Bible is clear "whatever a man sows, that is what he will also reap" (Galatians 6:7). God clearly states what the nations do to Abraham's seed, will be done to them. "I will bless those who bless you, and I will curse him who curses you" (Genesis 12:3). This is a universal principle: No one avoids judgment– "Be sure your sin will find you out" (Numbers 32:23).

WHO'S YOUR LAMB?

Judgment would come upon every home– except those who followed God's "plague prevention" program, centering around the blood of the lamb.

> Your lamb shall be an unblemished male a year old; you may take it from the sheep or from the goats. And you shall keep it until the fourteenth day of the same month, then the whole assembly of the congregation of Israel is to kill it at twilight. Moreover, they shall take some of the blood and put it on the two doorposts and on the lintel of the houses in which they eat it. (Exodus 12:5-7)

In Exodus 12 the lamb to be sacrificed was to be selected on the tenth day of the month and kept until the fourteenth day of the month. Why? During that time the lamb had to be inspected to certify that it was without blemish.

For redemption, the lamb had to be flawless. Though the Israelites were anxious to flee bondage, it was better to take the time to insure having a perfect lamb for redemption, than to merely make a quick escape from their circumstances.

Yeshua entered Jerusalem on the tenth of the month as a Passover lamb was being selected for each family. During this time Yeshua was inspected, questioned, interrogated, and then He was tortured. On the fourteenth of the month the head of the Roman government declared, "I find no fault in Him" (Luke 23:4).

Yeshua was recognized and declared to be the perfect Passover Lamb. He died for our redemption from the bondage of sin.

A PERSONAL IDENTIFICATION

Note the progressive order regarding the lamb in Exodus 12. We read that the Israelites were to select *a* lamb from the flock. Once selected, it is referred to as "*the* lamb." After it is inspected for several days, it becomes "*your* lamb," and only then it is killed (Exodus 12:3-6).

When you first realize your need for a Savior you may select Yeshua as *a* lamb. In the midst of the storms of an unredeemed life, it seems like any savior will do, like any port in a storm. Once you have chosen Him, you see that He is in fact *the* Lamb, the Savior, indeed the Lord! However, to be redeemed you must personally inspect Him and realize that He is *your* Lamb, *your* Savior, and *your* Lord. It is in personally placing your trust in Him that you might see His salvation for you from your sins.

A PRIVATE IDENTIFICATION

In Exodus 12:8-9, Passover was also a time to be continuously nourished in the redemption of the Lamb. Three specific items were to be eaten at the meal:

1. *The bitter herbs:* They remind us of the purpose of redemption. Never forget the pain of a life in bondage to sin before redemption came. Also remember the bitterness of pain endured by Messiah that we might live.

2. *The matzah:* It is unleavened bread which reminds us of the results of redemption. As yeast (or leaven) represents a type of sin (pride and unbelief), so unleavened bread speaks of the sin-cleansed life that Messiah brings. He is "the Lamb of God who takes away the sin of the world" (John 1:29).

3. *The lamb*: It reminds us of the price of redemption— the sacrifice of Messiah. Thus, Passover reminds us to consider privately in our souls the pain, the price, and the results of Messiah's redemption.

A PUBLIC IDENTIFICATION

The death of the Lamb was not the last word on the subject of redemption from bondage. Those who trusted in the lamb were to place the blood on the outside of their doors. This may strike some of us as rather strange. Why put blood on the door?

Again, in Exodus 12:13 we see the reason: "The blood will be a sign for you... and when I see the blood I will pass over you and the judgment shall not come upon you." Redemption from judgment would come only by the applied blood of the Lamb.

Why would God want the Israelites to apply blood for Him to see? It is not that God forgot where they were living! Rather, God wanted to redeem a people who would trust His way of salvation. He was going to redeem a people not merely of the flesh, but a people of faith.

Think about it: what really was the essential spiritual difference between the Hebrew and the Egyptian at that first Passover? Is it a difference in niceness, or better works? To put it another way, what is the difference between a believer in Yeshua and a non-believer? The difference is the blood of the Lamb. Only those who respond in faith and apply the Lamb's blood on the doorpost of their heart are redeemed from bondage today. Whether you are Jewish or Gentile, it is only by personally trusting in Messiah's blood atonement that you are secured from a far worse judgment.

God wants us to publicly identify with the Lamb of God, Messiah Yeshua. "But isn't faith supposed to be a personal matter?" Yes, but not only a personal matter. Those who have confidence in His atonement confess His redemption as well.

Yeshua said in Matthew 10:32-33,

Therefore everyone who confesses Me before men,
I will also confess him before My Father who is in

heaven. But whoever denies Me before men, I will also deny him before My Father who is in heaven.

Freedom from bondage is also freedom from fear's domination of your life. Have you confessed Yeshua and experienced the freedom He brings? Scripture says, "If the Son therefore shall make you free, ye shall be free indeed" (John 8:36).

A PROMPT IDENTIFICATION

In Exodus 12:10-11, the Lord exhorted the people to respond quickly to the opportunity for redemption. They were not to delay by "leaving the lamb over until morning" (Exodus 12:10). Identifying with the Lamb demands an urgent responsiveness. Three times the Scripture exhorts us to leave nothing over till morning:

1. *Manna in the wilderness*: The manna reminds us of the daily bread of the Word of God. Do not neglect the word God has for you today— today's word is for today's needs in your soul (Exodus 16:19).

2. *Thanksgiving offering*: The thanksgiving offering in Leviticus 7:15 speaks of our need to respond in faith, with thanksgiving today. It is not faith to wait and see how it turns out before you give thanks to the Lord. We know by faith that "all things work together for good to those that love God and are the called according to His purpose" (Romans 8:28). Therefore, we are to "give thanks in all things for this is the will of God for us in Messiah Yeshua" (1 Thessalonians 5:18).

3. *The Lamb during the first Passover*: Redemption in the Lamb is for today. We are to "seek the Lord while He may be found" (Isaiah 55:6).

There are to be no spiritual leftovers. Redemption will not wait. The people were to eat with a prompt readiness, hence they ate with their sandals on their feet and their loins girded and their staff in their hands (Exodus 12:11). Though it may have looked like the first "to go" meal, this was not "fast food" or "take out." They were ready to go on a moment's notice, at the Lord's command, living for and looking toward their deliverance.

We are to live like we are going somewhere, even being ready to leave in the "twinkling of an eye" (1 Corinthians 15:52). "No man knows the day or the hour" of Messiah's return. He will come as "a thief in the night" (Matthew 24:36). Those redeemed in the Lamb are ready to leave, for they no longer live for this world and its bondage, but for heaven and God's glory. When your neighbors see your life, is it a testimony that you are redeemed, and ready to leave?

THE LAMB THROUGH SCRIPTURES

For followers of Yeshua, Passover not only reminds us of the Exodus story, but how redemption in the Lamb affects our lives now and even into eternity. In the Scriptures God progressively reveals this truth of the Lamb of redemption so we may grow into the image of the Son: the Lamb of God.

A LAMB FOR THE PERSON

Though sacrifices are alluded to in Genesis 3:21 and firstlings of the flock are mentioned for sacrifice, it is not until Genesis 22:7 that a lamb for sacrifice is first specifically mentioned in Scripture. In the narrative, God commanded Abraham to offer his only son as a sacrifice: "He said, 'Take your son, your only son Isaac, whom you love, and go to the land of Moriah, and offer him there as a burnt offering on one of the mountains of which I shall tell you'" (Genesis 22:2). The rabbis teach that this was the final exam of ten tests, and it was no easy trial, but went to the very core of Abraham's being. This test demanded heart rending commitment and trust on Abraham's part. Isaac was a gift from God to Abraham and Sarah. So like Abraham, we must ask ourselves, "Do I love the gift more that the Giver? Do I trust God for His plan?"

This was Abraham's dilemma: Isaac was the child of promise through whom all the nations of the world would be blessed. If he sacrificed Isaac, what would happen to God's plan? Rather than attempting to figure out how God was going to accomplish His will, Abraham simply trusted and obeyed, and with confidence stated, "I and the boy will go over there and worship and come again to you" (Genesis 22:5). "I and the child will return!" Abraham knew there was no "plan B" with God. Thus, Hebrews reveals to us, "By faith, Abraham, being tested, offered up Isaac... concluding that God is able to raise up even from the dead. Figuratively speaking, he also did receive him back from the dead" (Hebrews 11:17-19). If God can bring forth life from Sarah's dead womb, He can raise the dead back to life.

Regarding Isaac carrying the wood for the burnt offering up the mountain, the rabbis teach that Isaac was "like a man carrying his cross" (Genesis Rabbah 56:3). Though Isaac was submitted to his father's will, he was aware of the circumstances. Isaac asks, "My father... Behold the fire and the wood: but where is the lamb for a burnt offering?" (Genesis 22:7). Where is the lamb? Isaac, you are the lamb. Could Isaac trust his father? Yes he could! As parents, our children should be able to have the same confidence in us: "If my father follows God, I will follow my father."

In response to Isaac's question Abraham said, "My son, God will provide himself a lamb for a burnt offering." So they went both of them together (Genesis 22:8). Abraham and Isaac went willingly to the place of sacrifice, confident that God would work out the details: and He did. At just the right time, God halted Abraham, and provided a sacrifice "in the place of his son Isaac" (Genesis 22:10-13). Why did God require a sacrifice lamb for Isaac? Even though he was a good, obedient son, the requirement for sacrifice pointed to the truth that even the "best" of people need the Lamb. We often think of Messiah's sacrifice as sufficient for the worst of people, but "all have sinned and have fallen short of the glory of God" (Romans 3:32).

That is why Messiah came to Israel. Messiah came to the only people who had the truth of Scripture, the Torah. Thus, they were the most moral of all people in the world. But even with the Torah, we see that the best of people need the Lamb. All are accountable before God; all have sinned. So we see at the first reference of a lamb for sacrifice that there is a Lamb for the person.

A LAMB FOR THE FAMILY

When the first Passover took place during Israel's exodus from Egypt the lamb was required. We saw how God told Moses that the blood of the lamb would be a sign for the "houses where you are" (Exodus 12:13). The lamb would insure the safety of each Israelite family:

They shall take to them every man a lamb, according
to the house of their fathers, a lamb for a house. And if
the household is too little for the lamb, let him and his
neighbor next unto his house take it according to the
number of the souls. (Exodus 12:3-4)

Please note that it says, "if the household is too little
for the lamb." The household may be too little for the
lamb, but the lamb is always more than enough for the
household!

The Lamb is God's sufficiency for the family and
desperately needed. Today the family is under spiritual
assault like never before. What will secure our family and
children? One of the families I have been ministering to
received shocking news: their teenage daughter ran away
from home. Saddest of all was the note she left, "Dad, I
feel so guilty for all you've done for me. I feel so ashamed
for my mistakes even after all you've done for me and the
family." It was true; he had worked night and day that they
might have a roof over their heads and food on the table,
but he had not given them the most important thing they
needed: the Lamb of God.

The Lamb is sufficient and more than enough for any
household. It is not your hard work, your income, or your
sacrifice that will secure your family– it is His sacrifice.
Your family needs the Lamb of God, and thankfully there
is more than enough for your family. Parents, the best
service you can provide for your family is to share the
Lamb of God with them. There is a Lamb for the family.

A LAMB FOR ISRAEL

In the days of the prophets, Israel had become more
than just families and tribes, but a nation. With greater
size, comes greater sin. What would meet the needs of this

people? Isaiah wrote that Messiah would be the Prince of Peace (Isaiah 9:6-7), and the prophet recognized that even he and his people needed the Lamb. Isaiah 53:6-8 says:

> All we like sheep have gone astray; we have turned every one to his own way; and the Lord has laid on him the iniquity of us all. He was oppressed, and he was afflicted, yet he opened not his mouth: he is brought as a lamb to the slaughter, and as a sheep before her shearers is dumb, so he opened not his mouth... He was cut off from the land of living for the transgression of my people was he stricken.

Yeshua went willingly, "as a lamb led to the slaughter" to the place of sacrifice, "for the transgressions of my people." There is not only a lamb for the person, and a lamb for the family, but there is a lamb for the people.

In Luke 19:41-42, we see Yeshua on the Mount of Olives approaching Jerusalem amid thousands hailing Him as the Messiah of Israel. Yet strangely Yeshua is weeping. Why? He is fulfilling the prophecy of Zechariah,

> Rejoice greatly, O daughter of Zion! Shout in triumph, O daughter of Jerusalem! Behold, your King is coming to you; He is just and endowed with salvation, humble, and mounted on a donkey, even on a colt, the foal of a donkey. (Zechariah 9:9)

Israel's King presents Himself for who He really is, but He knows that He will be rejected by the people He loves. Thus He wept, "If you had known, even you, at least in this your day, the things which belong unto your peace. But now they are hidden from your eyes" (Luke 19:42). Today Israel longs for peace, makes deals for peace, gives land for peace, yet peace will not come until the Prince of Peace is honored. Even so, in the midst of the world's troubles, Israeli and Palestinian, Jew and Gentile, are finding peace in Messiah and with one another. Nevertheless, there are many that need to hear, and Messiah weeps still. The best way to bless Israel is to share the Lamb.

A LAMB FOR THE WORLD

As we move along with God into the New Covenant we begin to understand what this world needs: Messiah! Amongst governments and in the media 'world peace' is a frequent topic. In our world's efforts to bring about peace, one factor is often overlooked: sin. This world does not possess the power or the wisdom to deal with sin.

In the New Covenant we read, "Behold, the Lamb of God who takes away the sin of the world" (John 1:29). There is no wisdom for attaining peace without purity from sin. We need "wisdom from above [which] is first pure then peaceable" (James 3:17).

While traveling around Europe, I travel light to travel right. Yet sometimes I travel too light, and run out of socks. In a store I tried to explain my foot size. The sales person said that my struggle to explain my foot size will not be necessary— one size fits all. That is exactly what I am trying to tell everyone as well!

God has provided what the whole world needs— forgiveness of sins by faith in Messiah— and one size fits all. The best fit for the greatest need of this world is the Lamb of God, and the best news we can share with the world is the Good News. There is a Lamb for the world.

A LAMB FOR ETERNITY

In the book of Revelation, John describes how he saw a "strong angel proclaiming with a loud voice, 'Who is worthy to open the book, and to loose the seals thereof?'" John then tells us how he wept because no one was found worthy to open the book.

> One of the elders said to me, "Weep not: behold, the Lion of the tribe of Judah, the Root of David, hath prevailed to open the book, and to loose the seven seals thereof." (Revelation 5:5)

John turned and saw not a lion, but a lamb standing as though slain, and then tells how he saw and heard all creation saying with a loud voice, "Worthy is the Lamb that was slain to receive power, and riches, and wisdom, and strength, and honor, and glory, and blessing... unto Him that sits upon the throne and unto the Lamb for ever and ever" (Revelation 5:12). There is a Lamb for eternity!

What will secure your life forever? Is it that house, car, or career that you have invested your life in? I often tell the story of the Microsoft investor who was asked, "If you knew before what you know now, what would you have done differently then?" He answered, "I would have invested more; I would have invested everything!" If you were to ask that same question to a resident of Heaven, they would also say, "I would have invested more of my time, talent, and treasure in service for the Lamb" Yes, those who are growing into maturity live out the eternal values of Heaven as they live their lives on earth.

God is committed to growing us into His love and life through concern for the individual, the family, the nation, the world and living with eternity in view. There every tribe and nation will praise Him. All believers from all ages, Jew and Gentile, will be there. Will you be there? The Lord wants you there, for there He has provided a Lamb for eternity. Trust in the Lamb!

The centerpiece of the redemptive program of God is found in the Passover redemption (John 1:29; 1 Corinthians 5:7). Yeshua fulfills God's prescribed type of Messiah– the Lamb being the representation of our spiritual connection with God in every detail. What makes for a life of spiritual freedom as opposed to a life of spiritual bondage? It is in our identification with the Lamb.

An unblemished lamb had to be slain and its blood placed on the door of Israelite homes. Why was God looking for a sign? Because He was not going to redeem a people merely of the flesh, but of faith. If the Egyptians had obeyed and placed the blood on their doors, God would have spared them as well. Conversely, if the Hebrews did not apply the blood to their doors, judgment would have come.

The blood applied as the Scriptures prescribe makes for a sign of redemption that speaks of a greater redemption from a far more terrible judgment. This sign in Hebrew is 'ot, which refers to a miraculous sign. This sign takes our attention through the Scriptures:

✡ 1000 BCE: We read in Psalm 22 a description of one being crucified which was not a form a execution until the Romans came to power 1000 years later. But here we have a clear portrayal of how Messiah would die. "They pierced My hands and My feet" (Psalm 22:16).

✡ 700 BCE: Isaiah describes Messiah's identification with the Passover lamb in His death. "He was led as a lamb to the slaughter" (Isaiah 53:7).

✡ 30 CE: At Golgotha, or Calvary Messiah Yeshua, the true Lamb of God, was nailed to the cross (executioner's stake) and God fulfilled His sign and promise for our eternal redemption.

REDEEMED BY FAITH

Whether it was Abraham, Moses, David, or Isaiah, people have always been redeemed the same way at all times– by faith (Genesis 15:6). Prior to Messiah's coming, people had faith that anticipated what God would provide. Since Messiah's coming, people have faith that appropriates what God has provided: all with the same faith trusting in Yeshua, the centerpiece of history.

Since the Temple's destruction in AD 70 there have been no sacrifices by our people. Thus, the shankbone of a lamb (zoro'ah) is kept on the seder plate as a reminder of the last and final sacrifice for our redemption, the Lamb.

DO THIS IN REMEMBRANCE OF ME

At the end of a delicious meal the children look for the hidden Afikomen, and collect their reward from the head of the house for finding it. Do you remember the one bag with three pieces of matzah, and how the middle one alone is taken out and covered to be found after the meal? The Afikomen, in a way, illustrates our great salvation.

One of the names of Messiah is the Coming One (Psalm 118:26; Matthew 23:39); this is like Afikomen, the "one that comes after." Messiah, the Son of God, the second person of the Tri-unity (the middle piece), came in the flesh and died for our sins. He was wrapped in a shroud, buried until the third day. Then He was raised bodily from the dead, giving gifts to the sons of men. Everyone who finds Him, all who trust in Him, all who lay hold of Him by faith, receive not merely a reward from the head of the house, but the great gift of God– eternal life, forgiveness of sins, and a relationship with God forever. The Triune God of Israel has come to our aid.

After rewarding the finder of the *afikomen*, the head of the house takes this broken piece of *matzah* and breaks off a small piece for each person around the table. All the participants are reminded that God has broken their bondage and redeemed them at Passover. Since it is the last item eaten in the meal, it is a further reminder of the Passover lamb, the final sacrifice for redemption. Along with this *afikomen,* we partake of the third cup, called the Cup of Redemption. It is this broken *matzah* and third cup that Messiah also utilized to institute what has come to be called "the Lord's Supper."

> And while they were eating, Yeshua took some bread, and after a blessing, He broke it and gave it to the disciples, and said, "Take, eat; this is My body." (Matthew 26:26)

Here, then, the disciples would be drawn to the great provision that God has made for our salvation: the Lamb of God, who is also our Bread of Life. The traditional blessing over the bread would be recited:

Baruch Atah Adonai Eloheinu Melech ha-Olam
Ha-motzti lechem min ha'aretz.

Blessed are you, O Lord our God, King of the Universe,
Who brings forth bread from the ground.

Although Messiah would die for sins as the Lamb,
as the Bread of Life He would be brought forth from the
ground through His resurrection, as we will consider in
the next chapter.

Traditionally, at the third cup, we look at the deep red
color of the fruit of the vine, remembering that it is the
Cup of Redemption and think of the blood of the Lamb.
Yeshua gave a profound new significance to this cup. For
those disciples who sat around the table with Him, even
as his use of the bread was suprising, this must have been
shocking.

Likewise He also took the cup after supper, saying,
"This cup is the New Covenant in My blood, which is
shed for you. (Luke 22:20)

The New Covenant? The disciples would be familiar
with the prophecy of the New Covenant, promised by
God through Jeremiah in chapter 31:

Behold, the days are coming," says the LORD, "when
I will make a New Covenant with the house of Israel
and with the house of Judah. Not according to the
covenant that I made with their fathers in the day that
I took them by the hand to lead them out of the land
of Egypt, My covenant which they broke, though I was
a husband to them," says the LORD. "But this is the
covenant that I will make with the house of Israel after

those days," says the LORD: 'I will put My law in their minds, and write it on their hearts; and I will be their God, and they shall be My people. No more shall every man teach his neighbor, and every man his brother, saying, 'Know the LORD', for they all shall know Me, from the least of them to the greatest of them,'" says the LORD. "For I will forgive their iniquity, and their sin I will remember no more." (Jeremiah 31:31-34)

This bread and third cup remind us of the eternal covenant relationship we have with our God. We know Him, not merely know about Him. To know Him is relationship; to merely know about Him is religion. Yeshua said:

And this is eternal life, that they may know You, the only true God, and Yeshua the Messiah whom You have sent. (John 17:3)

But how do we know Him? It is not at the third cup that we come to know Him. You could say that it is by way of the first two cups:

✡ At the first cup the broken *Afikomen* pictured that God would provide for our redemption. We could never redeem ourselves, but God alone would provide the lamb. So Messiah, the Lamb of God, has been provided for our eternal redemption.

✡ At the second cup we recognized that this lamb was not only to be slain, but that the blood had to be applied to the door. If all the lambs in Egypt were slain but the blood was not applied, there would have been no Passover, and no redemption. So the fact that Messiah has been slain for our redemption does us no good unless the blood has been applied. By trusting in Messiah's sacrifice we apply His blood, by faith, as atonement on our heart's door.

This is how we come to the third cup, the place of remembering the relationship we have by faith in Messiah, the provision of God.

HALLELUJAH!

In many traditional homes the Cup of *Hallel,* or "Praise," is referred to as Elijah's Cup. This cup calls us to praise God as we remember all that He has done for us. In remembering, we also proclaim and rejoice in the true meaning of Passover. The head of the house sits opposite an empty seat traditionally left for Elijah the Prophet. Traditionally, Elijah is expected to arrive at Passover preceding and proclaiming the Coming One, that is, the Messiah Himself. Where did such an idea originate? This tradition is taken from the book of Malachi. In Malachi 3:1 we read:

> "Behold, I send My messenger, and he will prepare the way before Me. And the Lord, whom you seek, will suddenly come to His temple, even the Messenger of the covenant, in whom you delight. Behold, He is coming," says the LORD of hosts.

In the New Covenant, John the Baptizer came in the "spirit and power of Elijah" (Luke 1:17). When he saw Messiah coming he heralded, "Behold the Lamb of God, who takes away the sin of the world" (John 1:29).

At this time it is recognized that the place and seat left open for Elijah remains empty, and that he will not come this year, and therefore Messiah will not come this year. They must wait another year for Messiah, the Prince of Peace, to bring them to Jerusalem, the city of peace. In some homes that only know tradition and ritual, the Seder ends not with praise, but rather with a lament.

The saying, "next year in Jerusalem" (*Lashana Haba'ah birushalayim*), refers to the fact that for those without redemption in Messiah, they must wait another year for Hope to arrive. But for the redeemed who know the Lord, we end with rejoicing and praise. Messiah *has* come, fulfilled the requirements of the Law, fulfilled the need of the Passover Lamb, and obtained eternal life for all who will believe in Him. Having eternal life *now*, we look forward with confidence for Messiah's return to bring us to the New Jerusalem. Therefore, let us go forth as God's heralds declaring the ultimate Passover message: "Behold! The Lamb of God who takes away the sin of the world" (John 1:29).

OUR HUMBLE KING

When the Temple stood, multitudes of Jewish pilgrims came up to Jerusalem to celebrate Passover.[5] But the week before Yeshua came to die was a Passover not like any other. We read that when He was coming into Jerusalem, crowds of people came out to greet Him. They took the branches of the palm trees and began to shout, "Hosanna!

---

[5] Of the seven appointments described in Leviticus 23, three– Passover, Pentecost, and Booths– were regarded as Pilgrim Feasts. These special celebrations required all males to appear "before the LORD," first at the Tabernacle, and later at the Temple in Jerusalem (Exodus 23:17; 34:23; Deuteronomy 16:16). Messiah and the Apostles made the most of this feature (see also chapters 4 and 7).

Blessed is He who comes in the Name of the Lord, even the King of Israel" (John 12:12-13). This was prophesied by Zechariah, "Rejoice greatly, O daughter of Zion! Shout in triumph, O daughter of Jerusalem! Behold, your King is coming to you; He is just and endowed with salvation, humble and mounted on a donkey" (Zechariah 9:9).

This event is traditionally called Palm Sunday. Why did the people wave palm branches? To better understand this Jewish event, we need to understand the mind-set of first century Jewish pilgrims. Waving palm branches on Passover is not a known Jewish custom. The only time that branches are waved is on the Feast of Booths (*Sukkot*), a holiday we will look at in chapter seven. This fall holiday pictures King Messiah reigning in the Kingdom, with the nations from the entire world coming to worship Him. During that feast, a cluster of branches made up of palm, willow, and myrtle (called the *lulav* in Hebrew) is waved to glorify God and recognize Him as ruler over the whole world (Leviticus 23:40).

If palm branches were to be waved at Booths to symbolize the rulership of the Lord, then why were they waved when Yeshua entered Jerusalem at Passover? Traditionally, the rabbis taught:

> Whatever time of year the Messiah was to appear the Jews were to greet and hail Him by taking up the Lulav clusters and singing Hosannas to Him as the Holy One of Israel. (Peskita de Rab Kahana, 27:3)

Thus by waving the *lulavs* the Jewish people were recognizing their Messiah and King. Though called Palm Sunday, interestingly, John is the only writer that mentions palm branches being waved. In Matthew 21:8

the tender branches of the willow are noted and in Mark 11:8 leafy branches like the myrtle are mentioned. The three accounts taken together give a picture of the *lulav* being waved in prophetic recognition. The true King of kings, Yeshua the Messiah had arrived.

SELECTION OF THE LAMB

Remember how each Israelite household was to select a lamb on the tenth day of the month of Nisan, keeping the lamb till the fourteenth of that month? Why did they need to have this smelly little lamb running around their home for five days? "Your lamb shall be...unblemished" (Exodus 12:5) The lamb had to be *tamim,* or perfect, without blemish. It was necessary to inspect and observe to see if the lamb had any imperfection. Only then the lamb would be suitable for their redemptive sacrifice. At the same time as the families were selecting and inspecting their lamb for sacrifice, Yeshua presented Himself to Jerusalem as the humble Lamb of redemption. Mark 11:7 says, "Messiah Yeshua entered Jerusalem on the colt of a donkey." The New Covenant account indicates Yeshua's entrance was at the end of the day (Mark 11:11) on what would have been the tenth of the month. For the next several days, Yeshua was questioned, inspected and finally tortured by both Jewish and Roman authorities. By the fourteenth of the month, the fickle crowd quickly became a mob demanding Yeshua's death.

On that day— the day the lambs would be sacrificed for the Passover— Pilate, the regional head of Roman government, declared to them, "I find no fault in this man" (Luke 23:4). Acknowledged to be without blemish, Yeshua, our Passover Lamb was qualified and acceptable before God to be the sacrifice for our sins. However, though acceptable to God, He could not be sacrificed unless we rejected Him. Man's recognition of Yeshua's perfection was also the height of man's rejection of Him.

ACCEPTANCE OF THE KING

Though as a nation, Israel misunderstood the mission Messiah's first coming, one day, when the Lamb returns, He will be accepted by them. As it is written in Psalm 118:22, "The stone which the builders rejected shall become the chief of the corner." Also Zechariah 12:10 says, "they shall look upon Him whom they have pierced and mourn for Him as one mourns for his only son." On that day Israel as a nation will confess their sin of rejecting Messiah (Isaiah 53), and will be restored to God. As Romans 11:26 reiterates, "And so all Israel shall be saved: as it is written, 'There shall come out of Zion the Deliverer, and He shall turn away ungodliness from Jacob.'"

The day is coming when Yeshua will return and make what will truly be His triumphal entry. Messiah will reign and be glorified before all the nations (Matthew 25:31-32). We will forever glorify Him as the Lamb of Glory, even as we wave palm branches to signify His eternal majesty.

> After these things I looked, and behold, a great multitude which no one could number, of all nations, tribes, peoples, and tongues, standing before the throne and before the Lamb, clothed with white robes, with palm branches in their hands, and crying out with a loud voice, saying, "Salvation belongs to our God, who sits on the throne, and to the Lamb." (Revelation 7:9)

PASSOVER TODAY?

"This month shall be the beginning of months for you." Though traditional Judaism celebrates New Year's in the month of Tishrei (September-October), the biblical year was to begin during the Passover month of Nisan (March-April). Why did God want the year to begin with Passover? Because it is the redemption of God's people from bondage, and with God, all things begin with redemption.

Just as Passover was to mark Israel's redemptive beginning as a nation, so also the Lamb of God is your redemptive beginning when you believe in Yeshua: "if any person is in Messiah he is a new creation, old things have passed away, new things have come" (2 Corinthians 5:17).

The annual religious life of the Jewish people is to be based upon and oriented around Passover, in order to give us direction and stability. In the same way, our lives need to be based upon and oriented around redemption in Messiah, the Lamb of God. This is the sure foundation upon which all else will properly develop. It is this foundation that determines your security in any storm that may come throughout the year, and for the rest of your life.

Should believers today celebrate Passover? Consider: we know that it was understood and celebrated by all first-century believers. Paul could readily refer to Passover regarding spiritual areas of their lives because they all understood the meaning of it. The apostles' method of discipleship included teaching on the Feasts of Israel as the basis to understand the salvation experience (Passover,

Unleavened Bread and Firstfruits), their sanctification and growth in the Holy Spirit (Shavuot), and their future hope in Messiah (Trumpets, Day of Atonement and Tabernacles). I wonder if Paul could so easily use such references in our congregations and churches today. Paul and the other apostles might well be shocked at the lack of teaching and awareness regarding the biblical feasts among New Covenant congregations.

Moreover, Passover was relevant to all first century believers, and is a present picture of living the fulfilled life, not only a record of some ancient event. It is a constant reminder that we are no longer slaves in the bondage of sin because Messiah our Passover has been sacrificed. We are now free to follow and honor the Lord, and to live as new creations through Messiah's gracious atonement. It demonstrates that we are free from bondage: not free to foolishly do as we please, but free to follow God into the Land of Promise, and please Him in all aspects of our lives.

Paul was not telling the Corinthians that they should start keeping the Passover; they already were. Paul's point is that Passover should be celebrated properly; with a pure heart, otherwise it is a demonstration of hypocrisy. Paul understood that for believers, Passover was to be celebrated even as Moses taught. In 1 Corinthians 5:8, Paul uses the very same Greek word *heortazo* that is used for "celebrate" in the Septuagint, the Greek version of the *Tanakh*:

> Now this day will be a memorial to you, and you shall celebrate it as a feast to the LORD; throughout your generations you are to celebrate it as a permanent ordinance. (Exodus 12:14)

When Paul wrote to the Corinthians (and to us) "therefore let us celebrate the feast," he may have been thinking of this truth Moses shared with Israel. We can see clearly the Messianic fulfillment of the Passover in Yeshua, and we should celebrate it with an eternal perspective in our Messiah.

Some have suggested that Paul's use of "old leaven" might refer to the Jewish traditions. Thus as believers we would need to celebrate Passover only in the Lord's Supper, not as "the Jews do," for that would be "old leaven." But this idea is wrong. Leaven refers to moral corruption, not traditional observance. Of course, Yeshua himself celebrated Passover according to the traditional customs of the day, and He was not sinning in doing so.

"Old" in Greek is the same word used in Ephesians 4:22, "in reference to your former (old) manner of life." This "old yeast" (1 Corinthians 5:7) refers to the old self that is crucified with Messiah (Romans 6:6). Paul is not only telling believers to keep celebrating Passover, but to celebrate honoring Messiah, with the unleavened bread of sincerity and truth. We do not celebrate as in the former manner of life, with malice and wickedness, but with a pure attitude, and in accordance with the truth of God.

Are believers obligated to celebrate Passover in a traditional Jewish style, or according to a particular custom (many of which we have not even covered here)? Not at all: the Scriptures do not obligate a particular method of observance (Colossians 2:16-17).

However, biblically, celebrating Passover is normal for followers of Messiah. It gives insight on the spiritual truths of the Scriptures and is a healthy reminder to live a life pleasing to the Lord. New Covenant believers and congregations that do celebrate Passover and appreciate these "Jewish roots" are engaging in normal biblical practice. They are better equipped to recognize God's faithfulness, and how they do not support the root, but rather that it is the root which supports them (Romans 11:18).

Therefore, let us "keep the feast" this year and every year, not only so that we may better be discipled, but to invite our Jewish friends and family to Passover to hear the Good News that Messiah is "the Lamb of God, who takes away the sin of the world" (John 1:29).

QUESTIONS FOR PESACH:

1. What is a *seder*? What are the four cups?
2. Which verse in the Torah makes a sign a requirement for judgment to pass over the home? What was that sign?
3. Why did God require a sacrifice lamb for Isaac?
4. What would happen to the morally upright Jewish family who did not put the Lamb's blood on the door?
5. Why did the year begin with Passover?
6. Why should a follower of Messiah keep Passover?

59

GOD IS GAINING HIS PEOPLE

through

FIRSTFRUITS

CHAPTER 3

FIRSTFRUITS

ראשית

OUR RESURRECTED MESSIAH

IN THE TORAH

Then the LORD spoke to Moses, saying, "Speak to the
sons of Israel and say to them, 'When you enter the land
which I am going to give to you and reap its harvest,
then you shall bring in the sheaf of the firstfruits of
your harvest to the priest. He shall wave the sheaf
before the LORD for you to be accepted; on the day after
the Sabbath the priest shall wave it. Now on the day
when you wave the sheaf, you shall offer a male lamb
one year old without defect for a burnt offering to the
LORD. Its grain offering shall then be two-tenths of an
ephah of fine flour mixed with oil, an offering by fire to
the LORD for a soothing aroma, with its drink offering,
a fourth of a hin of wine. Until this same day, until you

have brought in the offering of your God, you shall eat neither bread nor roasted grain nor new growth. It is to be a perpetual statute throughout your generations in all your dwelling places.'" (Leviticus 23:9-14)

During the Feast of Unleavened Bread, at the end of the Sabbath which fell on Passover, people were delegated to go after sunset into different barley fields with sickles and obtain samples from each field. The barley for the Passover firstfruits offering (*reishit*) was laid together in a sheaf (literally an *omer*, or approximately four dry quarts) and brought to the court of the Temple. There, the grain was winnowed, parched, and bruised in a mortar.

The next morning after some incense had been sprinkled on the sheaf, the priest waved it before the Lord towards the four different points of the compass. He then took a part of the grain and threw it into the fire of the altar. Once the offering was accepted, the remainder of the harvest was then acceptable before God (Leviticus 23:11, 14).[6]

A TYPE OF THE RESURRECTION

We learned in the last chapter that Yeshua died as our Passover Lamb. That was not the end of the story, however! The Torah states that following the Sabbath after the Passover, the priest would present the firstfruits of the barley harvest to the Lord so that the rest of the harvest would be accepted. When the Temple stood, Firstfruits was observed the day after the Sabbath of the Passover. The Sunday after Passover would be the observance of Firstfruits.

---

[6] These observances could not be practiced after 70AD when the Temple was destroyed, though one practice using Firstfruits remained: "the counting of the *omer*" (Leviticus 23:15, see chapter 4, pp. 85-89)

Passover had begun when Yeshua died, and on the third day, early that Sunday morning, the priests were in the Temple offering up the firstfruits of the harvest. At this very time, our Messiah and High Priest was raised from the dead, offering up Himself as our atonement. In so doing, He became the firstfruits of the rest of the harvest of believers in Him. Therefore Paul writes:

> But now Messiah has been raised from the dead, the Firstfruits of those who are asleep. For since by a man came death, by a man also came the resurrection of the dead. For as in Adam all die, so also in Messiah all will be made alive. But each in his own order: Messiah the firstfruits, after that those who are Messiah's at His coming. (1 Corinthians 15:20-23)

On the first day of the week, Yeshua was raised bodily from the dead, to fulfill the symbolism of this yearly festival which falls within the days of Unleavened Bread. As Passover pictures Messiah as the Lamb who was slain, Firstfruits pictures Messiah who was 'raised up' as firstfruits, in whom alone those who are asleep will be "made alive." Firstfruits could not be celebrated apart from Passover; and Messiah's Resurrection can never be celebrated apart from His Passover sacrifice for us. This would be to separate the fruit from the root.

Firstfruits was celebrated only after entering the Promised Land (Leviticus 23:10). After all, how could it be celebrated in the wilderness where there is no harvest? So also, Messiah's resurrection speaks of life after and beyond this wilderness journey of struggle. This resurrection life will not be fully understood while in the bondage of sin.

In fact, it was not until after Firstfruits was observed that the new growth of grain could be eaten. Likewise, it was not until after Messiah's resurrection that believers could fully partake of the new growth, even the new life in Him. It was only after He had been raised and ascended to the Father that we received "the firstfruits of the Holy Spirit" (Romans 8:23).

FAITH IN THE FACTS

One day a man was passing a cemetery. One of the tombstones caught his attention. He paused to read the inscription on that tombstone. The words read: "I still live." Scratching his head, he said, "Well, if I was dead I'd be honest enough to admit it."

If you do not believe in the bodily resurrection of Messiah from the dead, you might think the same about the declaration that Yeshua lives. Even Yeshua's disciples had a difficult time understanding and believing in the bodily resurrection of their Messiah. In John 20:1-6 we meet three of Messiah's followers who visit the tomb early in the morning. Yeshua's friends could not come to the tomb on the Sabbath, because to make the journey then would have been to break the Sabbath law.

> Now on the first day of the week Mary Magdalene came early to the tomb, while it was still dark, and saw the stone already taken away from the tomb. So she ran and came to Simon Peter and to the other disciple whom Jesus loved, and said to them, "They have taken away the Lord out of the tomb, and we do not know where they have laid Him. So Peter and the other disciple went forth, and they were going to the tomb. (John 20:1-3)

In the Good News account of John, the author first mentions Miriam (Mary in some translations, but the name would have been Miriam in Hebrew, which became Maria in Greek; she is called Mary Magdalene because of the town where she was born, Magdala). In his account, John was filling in details the other Good News writers did not include. Miriam, a follower of Yeshua, had come to the tomb early on the first day of the week to honor Him. So it was early on Sunday morning when she arrived. The word used for "early" is *proi* in Greek. This was the technical word for the period from 3 a.m. to 6 a.m, the last of the four watches of the night.

Miriam became very upset to find that the immense stone covering the tomb was gone. Immediately she ran to Peter and John to let them know that, "They have taken away the Lord." But who are *they*, Miriam? She never quite says who *they* are, though later on she thinks maybe the gardener had something to do with it (John 20:15).

She may have initially thought that the Jewish authorities had taken away Yeshua's body, being not satisfied with just crucifying Him; they were inflicting further indignities on Him. Today, some who deny the resurrection have conjectured that someone took away the body. Many say that it was the disciples who stole the body of Yeshua. As we will see more fully it was impossible for these terrified disciples who deserted Him at His arrest to take the body of Yeshua. Could they overpower the Roman soldiers who were guarding the grave? Others say maybe grave robbers took the body. But back then, grave robbers looked for treasure, not bodies. The Jewish authorities would never have stolen, nor permitted the body of Yeshua to be taken– for that would only seem to confirm Yeshua's prediction of His resurrection.

Miriam judged by her experience and could not think of another explanation. Sometimes we are limiting our lives because we base it on our limited experience. We often forget that we serve God with whom all things are possible.

> The two were running together; and the other disciple ran ahead faster than Peter and came to the tomb first; and stooping to look in, he saw the linen wrappings lying there; but he did not go in. (John 20:4-5)

Both Peter and John ran to investigate the matter of the missing body of Yeshua. This was serious and demanded their immediate attention. But John, who was younger, outran Peter. Miriam was following, but far behind. "And so Simon Peter also came, following him, and entered the tomb" (John 20:6). Peter, who was bolder, enters the tomb to discover the facts of the matter while John initially remains outside looking in.

Faith in the resurrection is backed up by the evidence. We know that He was declared dead by professional Roman executioners, and also buried, entombed, enwrapped, and embalmed. "Nicodemus also came, bringing a mixture of myrrh and aloes, about a hundred pounds in weight. So they took the body of Yeshua and bound it in linen wrappings with the spices, as is the burial custom of the Jews" (John 19:39-40). Even if Yeshua was still alive when He was taken off the cross, He would have suffocated under the weight of the embalming spices and the tightness of the wrappings.

We also know that the tomb was totally secured by the stone, the soldiers, and the seal (Matthew 27:60; 28:65-66). Tombs in ancient times were not commonly closed by doors. In front of the opening was a groove in the ground; and in the groove ran a stone, circular like a cartwheel; and the stone was wheeled into position to close the opening. The stone would have been huge and would have been a physical impediment for several men to move. The stone that was rolled into that groove in front of the tomb opening, would have had to be rolled up the grooves incline in order to just open the tomb.

The soldiers would have proved to be a real obstacle for anyone, since the soldiers faced the death penalty if they failed their duty and allowed someone to disturb the grave. But beyond all the rest was the seal placed on the door of the tomb (Matthew 27:66). The seal represented the authority of Rome and would have meant capital punishment for anyone who would dare break the seal in an attempt to move the stone.

Then there is the witness of Yeshua's appearances, testified by numerous and various eyewitnesses (John 20:11, 19; 1 Corinthians 15:6; John 20:16; Matthew 28:9). This list included unexpected witnesses, such as his previously unbelieving brothers (1 Corinthians 15:7-9). Also, there was the witness of those things which certified His death: the stone removed, the soldiers scattered, and the seal broken. The frightened followers of Yeshua would have had neither the physical power nor the *chutzpah* ('nerve' in Yiddish) to take on Rome— not with their only hope apparently dead in the tomb!

Beside all these issues, two other specifics must be considered: the items remaining in the tomb. Like forensic detectives today, when Peter and John investigated the tomb's physical evidence, they saw the linen wrappings and the face-cloth. The body would have been literally encased by the spices in the grave wrappings. In order to get the body out of the wrappings, any mere mortal would have had to cut or tear away the wrappings. It would have been foolhardy for anyone to do it there at the tomb— not with the guards and other possible witnesses to their grave robbing. They would have to remove the enwrapped corpse first and then gone to a private area to take off the wrappings.

However, the grave clothes were there in the tomb and they were not cut or torn away; they were not even disheveled or disarranged.

John writes:

And he saw the linen wrappings lying there, and the face-cloth which had been on His head, not lying with the linen wrappings, but rolled up in a place by itself. (John 20:6-7)

The grave clothes did not look as if they had been put off or taken off; they were lying there in their regular folds as if the body of Yeshua had simply vanished out of them. The head wrapping like a detached ball from the rest of the wrappings had rolled up. The resurrection of Yeshua was by the power of God and as He would later be able to enter locked rooms, so He was able to just leave His wrappings. Did He roll the stone at the tomb's entrance to get out? No, He did not have to move the stone to get out, just like He did not have to tear apart His grave wrappings to get out of them. The stone had been supernaturally moved not to let Yeshua out, but to reveal that He was not there. He had risen, just as He said.

The meaning of the facts penetrated John's mind; he realized what had happened– "he saw and he believed" (John 20:8). They came concerned about Yeshua and left confident in Yeshua. The facts will do that. It may seem odd to those who do not have faith in the God of the Scriptures, but faith is based upon the reality of the object of faith. Before Peter or John ever had an experience of seeing the risen Messiah, they believed because of the facts.

Biblical faith is based on the truth, the facts about God; spiritual experience is to be a result of that faith not the cause of that faith.

WHOM ARE YOU SEEKING?

> But Miriam was standing outside the tomb weeping; and so, as she wept, she stooped and looked into the tomb; and she saw two angels in white sitting, one at the head and one at the feet, where the body of Yeshua had been lying. And they said to her, "Woman, why are you weeping?" She said to them, "Because they have taken away my Lord, and I do not know where they have laid Him."

Here we have quite a scene: John was rejoicing leaving the tomb, but Miriam at the tomb was still weeping. She hadn't looked at the evidence, but assumed that His body had been stolen, and she was wrong, painfully wrong.

> When she had said this, she turned around and saw Yeshua standing there, and did not know that it was Yeshua. Yeshua said to her, "Woman, why are you weeping? Whom are you seeking?" Supposing Him to be the gardener, she said to Him, "Sir, if you have carried Him away, tell me where you have laid Him, and I will take Him away. (John 20:11-15)

Assuming He was dead, and caught up in her own misery, Miriam could not recognize that the person talking to her was in fact the Messiah. She could not recognize Yeshua because He was supposed to be dead and mourned as a martyr— she was not looking for any facts to the contrary. I wonder if we sometimes miss seeing God's miracles and messengers because we too get caught up in our own misery.

Yeshua first repeats the angels' question, "Woman, why are you weeping?" There is a time to weep, but it was not then! Miriam wept because in her misery she assumed that Messiah's body had been taken. In her frustration she did not know what to do. Her tears were based on a false assumption, and without her Lord's words and promise of resurrection placed in the equation. Miriam did not have faith in the evidence which resulted in an reaction and even a denial of the resurrection facts.

So Yeshua then asked her, "Whom are you seeking?" This seems like a rather obvious question, but demands a more profound answer than the obvious. Yeshua's question was meant to have Miriam think through this matter more deeply.

"Whom do you seek?" equates to "What kind of Messiah do you seek?" During His earthly ministry there were a variety of seekers. For example, Scripture indicates that Judas Iscariot expected a different type of Messiah. Disappointed, he turned Yeshua in to the authorities because he considered Him to be a threat to the Jewish nation. Are we seeking a Biblical Messiah? Scripture declares Him to be *Ben Elohim*, the Son of God, and indeed the Mighty God (Isaiah 9:6). He would die, but as atonement for our sins, He would not stay dead!

Supposing that Yeshua is the gardener, she asks Him: "Sir, if you have carried Him away, tell me where you have laid Him, and I will take Him away" (John 20:15).

In the phrase "take Him away" there is the Greek word *airo* which means to raise, take up, or lift. Earlier in this chapter the stone was "taken away" (John 20:1). Miriam also thought others had "taken Him away" (John 20:2, 13). Now she was going to "take Him away" as well?

Miriam, are you going to carry all by yourself a 150-175 pound dead body with a hundred pounds of spices added to his body? Once more, in her sadness she may not have been thinking straight. But this same Greek word is also used in John 1:29, "Behold the Lamb of God that *takes away* the sin of the world." Again in John 10:18:

> No one has *taken* My life away from Me, but I lay it down on My own initiative. I have authority to lay it down, and I have authority to take it up again. This commandment I received from My Father.

Miriam was to discover that it is not what she can do for Messiah but what He will do for her. He takes away the sins of the world and your sins as well. What Messiah has done will *lift* you from the depths of despair and judgment. He died, but He vanquished death and was able to take back His life. His Resurrection means the forgiveness of our sins in Him.

Death is the ultimate weapon of the enemy; resurrection makes no compromise with death, but overthrows it. Messiah's resurrection is also the ultimate affirmation that creation matters, as do our physical bodies. The true resurrection defies the Gospel of Judas and other Gnostic writings which saw the body as irrelevant.

> Yeshua said to her, "Miriam!" She turned and said to Him in Hebrew, "Rabboni!" (which means, my Teacher) (John 20:16)

When Miriam heard her name in a familiar voice and manner she responded, "Rabboni." She responded in the dialect of her heart. Yeshua said to Miriam:

> Stop clinging to Me, for I have not yet ascended to the Father; but go to My brethren and say to them, "I ascend to My Father and your Father, and My God and your God." (John 20:17)

Some translate this verse, "*Do not touch Me*, for I have not yet ascended to the Father." There is a difficulty here for some since a few verses later Messiah invites Thomas to touch Him (John 20:27). In order to prove that He is not a ghost, but that He was resurrected bodily, He tells his disciples, "See my hands and my feet, that it is I myself; handle me and see; for a spirit has not flesh and bones, as you see that I have" (Luke 24:39). Also in Matthew, "they came up and took hold of his feet and worshipped Him"

(Matthew 28:9). So why does He say to Miriam do not touch Me and elsewhere He invites others to touch Him?

The New American Standard Version translates John 20:17, "*Stop clinging to Me.*" This is much closer to the intent of the Greek. The word translated touch or cling is the Greek word *hapto*, which means to hold, or to fasten. Upon seeing Him, Miriam probably grasped Him with the intent of not letting Him go again.

Yeshua's statement, "Do not [hold] me, for I have not yet ascended to the Father," sounds hard to understand, as if He was saying that He should not be impeded until after He had ascended. Why? At this point it is necessary to understand the Jewish context of Firstfruits and its fulfillment through Messiah. Yeshua was ascending to bring the firstfruits offering to heaven. As the Priest offered Firstfruits in the Temple, Yeshua as our High Priest *(Cohen HaGadol)* offered His atonement to His Father in heaven.

This is why Yeshua prophesied numerous times that He would be killed on Passover, be raised on the third day in order to bring the Firstfruits offering to the throne of grace. As Paul later writes on this same matter, "raised on the third day according to the Scriptures... Yeshua our Firstfruits from the dead" (1 Corinthians 15:4, 20).

We therefore have assurance that He is our Passover lamb who takes away the sin of the world because He is our Firstfruits that brings His atonement before God to remove our sins forever.

GO AND TELL

Yeshua further says to Miriam, "Go and tell my brethren" (John 20:17). Tell your brothers that the Firstfruits offering is with the Father; we are saved in Him. We need to proclaim the same truth as well– to all with ears to hear. He has risen the offering is made, all in Him are accepted.

Who are they, "My brethren"? They are the believers (John 20:18). This is the first time that He specifically calls them brethren. In His resurrection body Yeshua is still clothed in flesh, and therefore "is not ashamed to call us brethren" (Hebrews 2:11). In His resurrection, we are now His brethren, not mere disciples.

He calls us brother and friend; we call Him Master and Lord. These brethren were His followers– and also His deserters. And yet He calls them brethren– even Peter, who denied Him three times and deserted Him in His hour of need. What amazing grace for all who will believe. Because of His perfect firstfruits offering we have complete forgiveness, salvation and acceptance in that offering He made for us. Our failures do not end His victory.

Yeshua said to Miriam, "My Father and your Father, and My God and your God" (John 20:17). We are Yeshua's brethren by faith and because God is His Father He is our Father also. If you accept the message that the offering has been made– then because of His death, resurrection, and firstfruits offering we now share in His sonship.

> Those whom He foreknew, He also predestined to become conformed to the image of His Son, so that

He might be the firstborn among many brethren. (Romans 8:29)

The resurrection not only assures us that our sins are forgiven, but that we have a new relationship with the living God, we are children of God (*b'nai Elohim*). This is why John who wrote this account of Yeshua also proclaims in his first letter,

> See how great a love the Father has bestowed on us, that we would be called children of God; and *such* we are. (1 John 3:1)

Yeshua told her to "Go and tell," Miriam therefore declares, "I have seen the Lord" (John 20:18).

Indeed, he was seen on many occasion for the next forty days, and one day He will return and we shall see Him as well. Now we see Him with eyes of faith, "looking unto Yeshua the author and finisher of our faith" (Hebrews 12:2). Our faith does not mean knowing about Yeshua; it means knowing Him by trusting Him with the certainty of faith that Yeshua is alive.

He has been raised and we are assured of everlasting life in His finished work for our souls. In the assurance of the incontrovertible facts let us also go and declare the resurrection of Messiah and the forgiveness and salvation God has provided for all that will trust in Yeshua.

Firstfruits gave assurance that the rest of the harvest would be accepted: "He shall wave the sheaf before the LORD for you to be accepted" (Leviticus 23:11). Firstfruits as a type of our Savior's resurrection, guarantees our eternal hope in Messiah.

The offering of the wave-sheaf sanctified the whole harvest. Your eternal assurance of full acceptance by God is in Messiah's resurrection. His resurrection was proof that God accepted His sacrifice for our sins, "He who was delivered over because of our transgressions, and was raised because of our justification" (Romans 4:25). Thus the rest of the harvest may be accepted in Him as well! In Hebrew, the word accepted is *ratzui,* which means pleased, or delighted. God does not just barely accept us, but in Messiah, He is delighted and well pleased with us. He accepts us completely.

> Who is the one who condemns? Messiah Yeshua is He who died, yes, rather who was raised, who is at the right hand of God, who also intercedes for us. (Romans 8:34)

> And raised us up with Him, and seated us with Him in the heavenly places in Messiah Yeshua. (Ephesians 2:6)

> This hope we have as an anchor of the soul, a hope both sure and steadfast and one which enters within the veil, where Yeshua has entered as a forerunner for us. (Hebrews 6:19-20)

WHEN IS FIRSTFRUITS?

There are two different traditional Christian observances which are meant to observe the resurrection. First, there is weekly Sunday worship, the first day of the week. However, the day fulfilled by his resurrection, Firstfruits, is annual, not weekly. Also, as early as the second century, this day also came to be seen by anti-Jewish theologians as a replacement for the weekly Sabbath. So these purposes of celebrating the resurrection on one hand, and having a "new Sabbath" on the other, confuse more than they communicate.

Second, there is the yearly festival of Easter, which, after much historic debate, came to be observed by the western church in connection with the spring solstice and not in accordance with the Jewish Passover. Every so often, this also can lead to confusing results. For example, recently Easter fell at the end of March, and Passover did not arrive until the middle of April. In other words, Messiah's resurrection was observed three weeks *earlier* than His death! Little wonder, then, that Jewish people might find it impossible to relate Easter celebrations to a Jewish context.

We do not think that Firstfruits ever needed to be replaced. Numerous criticisms have been leveled against Easter, generally focusing on the "pagan roots" of its name, dating, and added customs (such as the Easter bunny). However, it is unnecessary for us to digress from what matters: the historical resurrection of Yeshua on Firstfruits. While it is clear that the Scripture does not force one into legalistic observance of a particular calendar, the reality of "Resurrection Sunday" is better appreciated in conjunction with the week of Passover, and identified with Firstfruits. It can only add greater meaning to our celebrations when the witness of history is kept in line with the witness of Scripture. Let us rejoice by exalting our Messiah, the Firstfruits of the Resurrection!

QUESTIONS FOR FIRSTFRUITS:

1. Why did the Israelites need to wait until they entered
   the Promised Land in order to observe Firstfruits?
   no harvest

2. Why did Miriam wait until Sunday morning to visit
   the tomb of Yeshua? *break law of Sabbath*

3. Name the obstacles one would have faced to steal the
   body of Messiah. *Soldiers, stone, weigh of body*
   grave clothes intact

4. What other facts support Messiah's resurrection?
   witness declared died of cross, embalming wrap spices

5. Why did Yeshua say to Miriam, "Stop clinging to *stone at door*
   me"? *for I will go to my Father*

6. Why is it important that Messiah arose on Firstfruits? *!!*
   sample of bring firstfruits offering to throne
   of Israel
   Matt 27 -

prayer list - Dennis Walker - Sunday 3:00 pray
her Dad at Kirby Pines
Aubrey - 2 chemos - mass has shrunk ½
Nathan healing
Jimmy Blount
B. 19 Cochran
Gretchen walk from Sat.
Jury & Mrs. Deaton
John - Barbara's brother in law

God Is Sanctifying
His People

through

שבועות
Shavuot

CHAPTER 4

THE FEAST OF PENTECOST

שבועות

THE OUTPOURING OF THE HOLY SPIRIT

IN THE NEW COVENANT

When the day of Pentecost had fully come, they were all together in one place. And suddenly there came from heaven a noise like a violent rushing wind, and it filled the whole house where they were sitting. And there appeared to them tongues as of fire distributing themselves, and they rested on each one of them. And they were all filled with the Holy Spirit and began to speak with other tongues, as the Spirit was giving them utterance. Now there were Jews living in Jerusalem, devout men from every nation under heaven. And when this sound occurred, the crowd came together, and were bewildered because each one of them was hearing them speak in his own language. They were amazed and astonished, saying, "Why, are not all these who are speaking Galileans? And how is it that we each hear them in our own language to which we were born? Parthians and Medes and Elamites, and residents of Mesopotamia, Judea and Cappadocia, Pontus and Asia, Phrygia and Pamphylia, Egypt and the districts of Libya around Cyrene, and visitors from Rome, both Jews and proselytes, Cretans and Arabs– we hear them in our own tongues speaking of the mighty deeds of God." (Acts 2:1-11)

Before we look at this feast in the Hebrew Scriptures, I wanted to skip ahead to the dynamic events "when the Day of Pentecost had fully come" (Acts 2:1). Pentecost means "fiftieth (day)," a word used to translate the Hebrew *Shavuot*. This holiday had come to its fulfillment fifty days after Messiah's resurrection.[7]

For the traditional Jewish community, Shavuot was first celebrated around the time of receiving the Torah at Mount Sinai, about fifty days after leaving Egypt (Exodus 19:1). Therefore, Shavuot is called "The Season of the Giving of the Law." It is also considered the spiritual birthday of Israel since the Torah brought twelve tribes together into one corporate people. From Shavuot's fulfillment in Acts we can also call it, "The Season of the Giving of the Spirit" since the Holy Spirit makes all believers, from many tribes, into one family in Messiah. Happy Birthday, Body of Messiah!

Luke, who wrote the book of Acts, was trained by his mentor Paul to understand the work of God in Messiah from a Biblically Jewish frame of reference.

---

[7] The Greek word used for 'fully come' is *sumpleroo*. Literally, "with fullness"; or "swamped." It is used in Luke 8:23 for a boat flooded with water. Shavuot was "fulfilled to overflowing."

Luke depicts the events of Acts 2 as a second "Mount Sinai experience." When the Law was given, there was fire and noise as God descended on Mount Sinai (Exodus 19:18-20). When the Spirit was given there was fire and noise as well (Acts 2:2-3). The rabbis comment in the Talmud that when the Torah was given at Mount Sinai, "Every single word that went forth from the Omnipotent was split up into seventy languages for the nations of the world."[8] When the Holy Spirit was given, men from every nation spoke in other languages as the Spirit enabled them: "Now there were Jews living in Jerusalem, devout men from every nation under heaven" (Acts 2:4-5).

This true fulfillment of Shavuot is also depicted in contrast to when the Torah was given at Mount Sinai. While the people waited for Moses to return back down from the mountain, an almost incredible chain of events began to transpire. Now, the Israelites had just witnessed the ten horrendous plagues upon Egypt, the opening of the Red Sea, and the supernatural revelation of God at Mt. Sinai. We had seen God work awesome wonders. In light of these events, the following verses are almost unbelievable:

> Now when the people saw that Moses delayed to come down from the mountain, the people assembled about Aaron, and said to him, "Come, make us a god who will go before us; as for this Moses, the man who brought us up from the land of Egypt, we do not know what has become of him." And Aaron said to them, "Tear off the gold rings which are in the ears of your wives, your sons, and your daughters, and bring them to me." Then all the people tore off the gold rings which were in their ears, and brought them to Aaron. And he took

[8] Sotah 32a, 36a, Shabbat 88b

this from their hand, and fashioned it with a graving tool, and made it into a molten calf; and they said, "This is your god, O Israel, who brought you up from the land of Egypt." (Exodus 32:1-4)

Tired of waiting for Moses, the people sinned by committing idolatry with a golden calf. Moses did make his way back down the mountain, but by then the party was in full swing. Upon Moses' arrival, God's verdict upon their sin was read, and the party was over. Sadly, judgment came at the giving of the Law, revealing the disasterous consequences to the idolaters' decisions:

> Then Moses stood in the gate of the camp, and said, "Whoever is for the LORD, come to me!" And all the sons of Levi gathered together to him. And he said to them, "Thus says the LORD, the God of Israel, 'Every man of you put his sword upon his thigh, and go back and forth from gate to gate in the camp, and kill every man his brother, and every man his friend, and every man his neighbor.'" So the sons of Levi did as Moses instructed, and about three thousand men of the people fell that day (Exodus 32:26-28).

Lest we forget, sin has a terrible end: 3,000 people died at the giving of God's righteous and holy Law. What a difference when Shavuot was fulfilled and the Holy Spirit (*Ruach HaKodesh*) was given. We read in Acts 2:41, "So then, those who had received his word were immersed; and that day there were added about three thousand souls." When the Spirit was given there were 3,000 people redeemed and made spiritually alive in Messiah. The law reveals sin that condemns us, but the Spirit reveals the Savior who saves us.

With this New Covenant perspective, let's now go back and understand more details about what Shavuot typified and promised to God's redeemed people.

THE TORAH TIMING OF SHAVUOT

> You shall also count for yourselves from the day after the Sabbath, from the day when you brought in the sheaf of the wave offering; there shall be seven complete Sabbaths. You shall count fifty days to the day after the seventh sabbath; then you shall present a new grain offering to the LORD. (Leviticus 23:15-17)

Of all the three major pilgrim festivals, Shavuot is unique. "Shavuot" actually means "Weeks." Why is it called this? It is not because the festival lasts for many weeks! Rather, it is called the Feast of Weeks because of the way you find out when it is to be celebrated. Unlike Passover and The Feast of Tabernacles, the Feast of Weeks is dateless.

In order to celebrate Shavuot you had to count "seven weeks" from "the day after the Sabbath" of the Passover, and the next day, the fiftieth day, would be Shavuot (Leviticus 23:15-16).

Why don't the Scriptures just give the date? In this fast paced "day-timer" controlled world we live in, we would have been inclined to say to Moses, "Forget counting fifty days, and just give me the date and I'll show up and worship!" No, you had to count fifty days regardless of how busy your schedule might be. Why?

In the same way, can you imagine if your mother never told you your birthday? Rather, she told you to celebrate it fifty days after the anniversary of your Uncle Murray's death. When you are very young, this might be okay, but in high school, it would be embarrassing not to know the date of your birth. "Hey Joel, when's your birthday?" "Well, it's fifty days after the day my Uncle Murray died." You would eventually run home, insisting on knowing the date of your birthday. Mom would reply, "It's fifty days after your uncle Murray died."

"But, Mom why do I have to count fifty days from Uncle Murray's death?"

"Because, your Uncle Murray left you his fortune and I never want you to forget your Uncle Murray!" Similarly, Israel was to count fifty days so that in order to celebrate Shavuot they would never forget Passover.

May it never be that Israel would reckon itself from the giving of the Law and not from the true foundation of their life as a people at Passover. Shavuot is traditionally remembered as a time when God made Israel one people in the Law. Nevertheless, it was Passover when God redeemed us from bondage and destruction through the blood of the Lamb.

Passover is to be the foundation and head of the year (Exodus 12:2). It celebrates Israel's redemption from bondage, and redemption is the foundation of our salvation. Thus the foundation of Israel's redemption was provided only in Passover, not Shavuot. Every year as Israel counted the weeks from Passover to Pentecost they remembered that their redemption as a people was found in the lamb of Passover.

Likewise, we are never to forget our Messiah who gave His life for us, and with that, the unspeakable riches of our new birth in Him. Like Israel's redemption from bondage, our foundation of faith as believers in Messiah Yeshua is forever tied to Passover and our redemption in the Lamb of God. We are not firstfruits to God just because we look to the Holy Spirit, but when we look to Yeshua as the true foundation for our spiritual lives. Through Him we are a firstfruits offering, for God's use only.

Every Shavuot, believers are compelled to remember Passover and the Passover Lamb, Yeshua. Though Pentecost is the 'birthday celebration' of the Body of Messiah when the Holy Spirit came, we are never to look to the Holy Spirit as the foundation of our faith either individually or as a body of believers. No matter how big or small our congregations may be, we are not secure in congregational size, wealth, or prestige. Our security is experienced only when we look to Yeshua as our foundation of faith. Our confidence is in the Lord and in Him alone. The Passover redemption of the believers reminds us each year that despite all that the world, the flesh and the devil may throw at us, we are secure in Messiah.

Passover was meant to be like the foundation of a house in a storm:

> Yeshua said, "Everyone then who hears these words of mine and acts on them will be like a wise man who built his house on the rock. The rain fell, the floods came, and the winds blew and beat on that house, but it did not fall, because it had been founded on the rock." (Matthew 7:24-25)

How strong is your foundation? Do you trust in someone or something besides the Lord (Jeremiah 17:5)?

If you are trusting in anything or anyone else, stop! Place your faith in His eternal atonement for your sins and receive new life in Yeshua, the Author and Finisher of our faith (Hebrews 12:2).

AN UNUSUAL SHAVUOT OFFERING

> You shall bring in from your dwelling places two loaves of bread for a wave offering, made of two-tenths of an ephah; they shall be of fine flour, baked with leaven as Firstfruits to the LORD. (Leviticus 23:17)

Here we find God's requirements for the Shavuot offering instructed through Moses to Israel. While the amount of flour ("two tenths of an ephah") is mentioned for other Feast days (e.g. Passover, Leviticus 23:13), an offering of "two loaves" is recorded only and distinctly on Shavuot. So we ought to ask: why two loaves?

The number "two" became a consistent picture for witness in the Scriptures; namely, it took two witnesses for an acceptable court testimony (Deuteronomy 19:15). This principle finds a variety of applications within the New Covenant. Congregations are not to allow an accusation to be made against an elder unless there are at least two witnesses (1 Tim. 5:19). Messiah sent out His disciples two at a time (Mark 6:7). There will be two witnesses against the anti-Messiah (Rev. 11:3-11). Also, in marriage there needs to be agreement between both spouses for prayer to be accepted by God (1 Peter 3:7). Without two witnesses, we have merely opinion.

What does this have to do with the two loaves? Note that the offering of the loaves accompanied several other sacrifices, including a peace offering (Lev 23: 19; cf. Lev. 7:9ff). This is crucial. When the Apostle Paul speaks to Gentiles at Ephesus, commenting on this offering (simply called "peace," just as the sin offering is called "sin"), he says:

> "But now in Messiah Yeshua you who are far off have been brought near by the blood of Messiah. For He Himself is our peace, who made both into one and broke down the barrier of the dividing wall...so that in Himself He might make the two into one new man, thus establishing peace" (Eph. 2:13-15).

Messiah is our peace offering, to unite Jews and Gentiles; so these two are witnesses to the reality of that fellowship that is found in Messiah. Since God desires to reach the whole world in the testimony of Messiah, there had to be two witnesses for the testimony to be credible. Faith in the God of Israel was never meant to be limited to one ethnicity. Therefore, God promised to save the Gentiles to join the testimony of the Jewish people, who were already a "witness" for the Lord (Isaiah 42:6-7; 43:10, 12; 44:8; 49:5-7).

This is why when the Day of Shavuot had "fully come," "both Jews and proselytes" are specifically mentioned as coming to faith at the same time (Acts 2:1, 10). A "proselyte" refers to a Gentile seeking the God of Israel. Luke is describing the two-loaves testimony– the body of Messiah.

Our witness is a spiritual unity and not based on cultural uniformity, where ethnic identity is lost. This unity is a result of a gracious work of Messiah in reconciling man to God. Thus, congregations should value the membership of both Jews and Gentiles as part of the unique New Covenant witness. Rather than being a problem or complication, the reality of Gentiles believing in a Jewish Messiah helps to demonstrate the validity of the Messianic witness.

I knew of one dynamic Jewish believer who was living in Israel for a time and served in the Israeli Army. He was faithfully witnessing for Messiah to all in his platoon. One night his squad was on patrol in Gaza when it was still under Israeli control. Suddenly they spotted a van parked where it wasn't expected to be. "Could it be a booby trap?" They all wondered. So they volunteered this believer— since, you know, he had faith— to go check out the van. As he carefully looked around the van he saw a Palestinian man coming out of a nearby house— and at that time it was after curfew! With his weapon drawn in front of him, he approached this Palestinian,

"Halt! What are you doing here at this hour?"

"I'm a Palestinian pastor of a local church and I was visiting one of the congregants," the man replied.

"Well, then, if you're a pastor, do you believe that Yeshua died for your sins?"

"Yes," the pastor replied.

"Do you believe that Messiah was raised from the dead?"

"Yes," the pastor again replied, wondering what was going on. No Israeli soldier had ever asked these questions of him before.

Finally, the soldier lowered his weapon and said, "Well, brother it is good to meet a fellow believer in Messiah!" They hugged and praised God together in the Gaza moonlight.

When he went back to his stunned, onlooking platoon, they asked, "What was that all about?" He smiled and said, "That Palestinian is my brother in Messiah. Yeshua made us one!"

This is the witness the world is looking for and the unity and fellowship the world so desperately needs. This is also the only hope for the Middle East and Israel. The reason there is unity is because both are looking to Messiah (Ephesians 2:14-16). The "two loaf witness" is the testimony of God's love in Yeshua for the whole world—"to the Jew first and also to the Gentile!"

LEAVEN IN THE LOAVES?

As we look at this unusual offering of two loaves of bread for Shavuot, a troubling question arises, "Why are the loaves made with leaven?" At the Feast of Passover the leaven issue was clear: no leaven was to be eaten during the week. If there was to be no leaven in the Passover bread, then why is leaven a part of Pentecost? To understand this, we first must understand how leaven is pictured in the Scriptures.

In the Tabernacle and the Temple, offerings with either leaven or honey could not be offered upon the altar as we read in Leviticus 2:11,

> No grain offering, which you bring to the LORD, shall be made with leaven, for you shall not offer up in smoke any leaven or any honey as an offering by fire to the LORD.

The leaven and honey are fermenting agents picturing natural fermentation which also illustrates the corruption of the world, and the corruption of souls through sin. The prophet Hosea likens adulterers to "leaven in the dough" (Hosea 7:4).

The New Covenant continues this theme regarding leaven. Messiah warns His followers of the hypocrisy, pride, and false teaching of the religious leaders of their day: "Beware of the leaven of the Pharisees, which is hypocrisy" (Luke 12:1). In 1 Corinthians Paul speaks to a congregation that tolerated sin in their midst. He addressed the issues of malice, wickedness, and unconfessed sin in their carnal fellowship (1 Corinthians 5:6-8).

Leaven is a clear picture of the corruption of sin. Understanding the biblical symbol of leaven can help us more accurately interpret certain Scriptures. In Matthew 13:33, Messiah is speaking of the mystery of the kingdom, "He spoke another parable to them, 'The kingdom of heaven is like leaven, which a woman took and hid in three pecks of flour until it was all leavened.'"

Many commentators think this speaks of the wonderful growth of the body of Messiah. But like the mustard tree parable before it, this too, speaks of the corrupted form of the kingdom that is leavened with false teaching and hypocrisy.

History contains episodes where after waging their wars, the so-called church actually marched captured pagan armies through a river, then declared them to be "baptized Christians." These so called Christians would then be allowed to continue in their pagan forms of worship. An example includes 'Mother worship,' the deification of the mother of Jesus and identifying her with the pagan goddess Ishtar– all done in the name of 'Christ' and 'church growth.' This is not a very sincere expression of faith. Is it any wonder that so many people today have a difficult time seeing the Jewish roots and context of our biblical faith? This parable in Matthew 13 cautions believers to live leaven-free lives.

Our service and growth in the Lord is to be without pride, hypocrisy, and wickedness that will lead to uselessness pictured as "wood, hay, and straw" (1 Corinthians 3:12, 13). The intimacy of our relationship with God is hindered while unconfessed sin remains in our hearts. We must "purge out this leaven" and admit it for what it is: sin. We then can be cleansed and walk closely with our God, experiencing again the joy of our salvation (Psalm 51:12).

Now that we understand the biblical symbolism of leaven we can begin to understand why the Shavuot offering of two loaves had to be "baked with leaven." Shavuot is a picture of the Body of Messiah: Jews and Gentiles. When the "fullness of Pentecost had come" there was an open invitation to all who would believe to be saved. It was in a sense a "come as you are" party. We all come to Messiah "as is"— with our sins. We are all moral failures, lost people in need of God's forgiveness, mercy, and grace. At Shavuot we are reminded that we are sinners without the Passover redemption. However, as we look to Messiah Yeshua and His salvation we find cleansing of our sins and a new life in Him.

At Pentecost we remember that He only saves sinners. A holy God cannot permit sin in His presence. Since the Scriptures make it plain that our sins have made a separation between us and God, how can a holy God accept a sinful person? (Isaiah 59:1-2)

In Leviticus 23:18-20 a bloody sin offering was also presented along with the two loaves: the offerings had to be presented together. Thus we see that sinful man is accepted before God only when the blood offering for sin is provided. The Pentecost offering was a picture of the gospel message, and it provided a perfect opportunity for believers to proclaim the Good News.

We all have fallen short of God's holy standards, and we can never come before the Holy God of Israel on our own merits. But God provided the atonement in Yeshua, our sin offering that we might be fully accepted in the Messiah.

Every Pentecost we are reminded that though we are fully accepted in the beloved, no matter how mature we get, we never outgrow our need for Him. "He must increase, but I must decrease" (John 3:30). Apart from Messiah we are but corrupted and damned sinners, but in Him we are saved and kept by God's grace in the eternal sufficiency of His blood atonement.

The offering was to be made with fine flour (Leviticus 23:17). "Fine flour" is the translation of the Hebrew word *solet*, meaning to strip, being crushed, or worn. In other words, all the chaff, lumps and inconsistencies are removed so that the flour is fine and consistent. Moreover, our consistency is to be conformed to the perfect character and spiritual image of Messiah (Romans 8:29). Chastening develops our consistency; it refines and works out the inconsistencies from our lives.

A picture from the ancient goldsmith may illustrate this refining work of God in our lives. Making pure gold from ore, the smelter heats the gold till the dross floats to the top. He draws off the impurities and looks into the molten ore. He repeats the process over and over: heating the ore, drawing off the dross and then looking into the ore. What is he looking for? He is looking for his own face reflected in the gold, which lets him know that all of the dross has been removed.

In the same way, our Lord develops us into fine flour through the chastening process of problems and trials, until the inconsistencies are removed and His character is consistently revealed in our lives. Problems can make us either better or bitter. Many people have a root of bitterness from miserable problems and tragic disappointments in life. What makes the difference? God's triumph and love is revealed in our testing and testimony when we look to the Lord. The salvation party is "come as you are"– but it is not "stay as you are" for we are transformed into His likeness. This offering could only be given if we reckoned our lives from the redemption. Look to Messiah: we are accepted in Him, being refined, firstfruits, and a testimony of unity in Yeshua, for He is the author and finisher of our faith.

HOW MANY FIRSTS?

As we read further regarding the special Shavuot meal offering, we see that it is also called "Firstfruits to the LORD" (Leviticus 23:17). However, we noted that there was already a firstfruits offering earlier during the week of Passover. Now there is a second firstfruits offering? At some point, one might think, shouldn't it be called "secondfruits"?

Not at all. Remember that the earlier firstfruits offering was presented the day after the Sabbath of Passover week (Leviticus 23:10-14). This was the firstfruits offering of the barley harvest, considered the poor man's food. The second firstfruits offering was from the wheat harvest (Exodus 34:22), the rich man's food (Psalm 81:16). As you will see, Messiah became poor that we might become spiritually rich in Him (2 Corinthians 8:9).

The earlier firstfruits offering pictured Messiah as our "firstfruits offering" from the dead (1 Corinthians 15:21-23). However the second firstfruits offering is a different picture altogether. This offering is a picture of the believers in Messiah made into His body at Shavuot in Acts 2.

We are a second firstfruits offering in Yeshua. This is referred to in the book of James 1:18, "In the exercise of His will He brought us forth by the word of truth, so that we would be a kind of firstfruits among His creatures."

As Yeshua is the Firstfruits offering of the resurrection, so also we are a firstfruits offering in His new creation, the Body of Messiah. We learn in Ephesians that Messiah is the Head, and we are the body (Ephesians 1:23; 4:15-16). When my son Josh was born, the midwife exclaimed, "I see the head." I did not need to ask if there was a body–if there is a head there is a body. Likewise as surely as Messiah was raised from the dead to be our Firstfruits offering, we must surely follow because where there is a Head there has to be a body. There had to be a second firstfruits offering.

By being given the firstfruits of the crop, the Lord was honored and recognized as the Provider. Thus firstfruits are for God's use only. The significance of believers being firstfruits is that we are to be totally dedicated to the Lord: we are for God's use only, set apart as saints unto Him.

At the first Shavuot the "firstfruits" were the people of Israel. In Jeremiah 2:3 God declares, "Israel was holy to the LORD, the firstfruits of His increase. All that devour him will offend; disaster will come upon them." Israel is not only God's "firstborn" of the nations (Exodus 4:22, 23), but is also the firstfruits of His increase, a nation called to be holy unto the Lord. This resulted in God's foreign policy of blessing or cursing those nations that interacted with Israel, "I will bless those that bless you [Israel], and curse those that curse you" (Genesis 12:3). This position of firstfruits also accounts for God's chastening upon our people, Israel, even as it is declared in Hosea 9:10, 17:

> I found Israel like grapes in the wilderness; I saw your fathers as the firstfruits on the fig tree in its first season. But they went to Baal Peor, and separated themselves to that shame; they became an abomination like the thing they loved. My God will cast them away, because they did not obey Him; and they shall be wanderers among the nations.

Along with the privileges of being God's firstfruits also came responsibilities, as we read in Luke 12:48, "to whom much is given, much is required." Consequently we are expected to live in such a way that the Lord is honored in all that we do. This is why the Holy Spirit was given– to empower all believers in Yeshua to follow Messiah.

The ultimate fulfillment of Shavuot firstfruits are New Covenant believers. When the Spirit of God came upon them in Acts 2, He made them into His firstfruits (James 1:18). Similarly, believers today are people of both privilege and responsibility to live faithfully for the Lord.

Through faith in Messiah we have eternal salvation and new life as children of God. What a privilege to have the enablement of the Holy Spirit (*Ruach HaKodesh*) to live dedicated and holy lives to the glory of God. Though there is "no condemnation to those who are in Messiah" (Romans 8:1), there is chastening and discipline from the Lord for every child of His that we might grow in righteousness (Hebrews 12:6-8). As believers we are to present ourselves for God's use only. We experience His spiritual blessings when we yield ourselves to the Lord, and in living for Him fulfill His purpose for us.

The final Shavuot firstfruits will be the 144,000 Jewish Tribulation believers. "These are the ones who follow the Lamb wherever He goes. These were redeemed from among men, being firstfruits to God and to the Lamb" (Revelation 14:4). Even in the midst of the darkest period of history, God will have His holy firstfruits as lights in the world to testify to all who will believe.

WHEN IS THE BIBLICAL FEAST OF SHAVUOT?

Many people desire to celebrate the Feast of Pentecost and want to know the actual Biblical date. Though the traditional Jewish community will celebrate Shavuot according to a traditional calculation, there is a difference of opinion on the matter. In the first century the Pharisees and Sadducees differed on the date that Shavuot was to be celebrated. The Scripture states that the Feast of Firstfruits was to be celebrated "the day after the Sabbath" (Leviticus 23:12, 15). Pentecost was then to be celebrated fifty days from that day. The question arose over which Sabbath does Firstfruits take place after: the Passover day, which is generally considered a Sabbath, or the regular seventh day Sabbath during the Passover week?

The Pharisees claimed the correct day was the day after the first day of Unleavened Bread, the sixteenth of Nisan. The Sadducees taught that the correct day was Sunday, the day after the weekly Sabbath. Since the writings of the Pharisees survived and developed into traditional Judaism, their opinion is accepted in modern Judaism. But who is biblically correct? Remember, the Scriptures state, "there shall be seven complete Sabbaths. You shall count fifty days to the day after the seventh Sabbath" (Leviticus 23:15-16).

For it to be the day after the seventh Shabbat, the initial Sabbath was the weekly Sabbath. So it would appear the Sadducees were right. However, since Shavuot is literally the Feast of Weeks, the Pharisees state that the word for Shabbat, should be interpreted to mean week and not the day itself. Amazingly, the year that Yeshua died, the sixteenth of Nisan fell on the Sunday, which is the day after the Sabbath for the Sadducees as well. God worked it out that neither group would have a reason not to recognize Yeshua as the Firstfruits of the Resurrection.

Following the regular offerings for the Feast of Pentecost (Leviticus 23:36), the people brought their own freewill offerings as the Lord had prospered them. They would then share with various people from all over the world and rejoice in the Lord (Acts 2:7-10). This would customarily last almost a week with the people reaching out to one another in love and fellowship. What a great opportunity for the believers and especially for Paul to reach out with the Good News as the Spirit of God gave them an open door. Yet we are accepted as we are because we look to Yeshua. In Him we have forgiveness, cleansing and full acceptance in the presence of God.

PAUL'S PRIORITY

> For Paul had decided to sail past Ephesus so that he would not have to spend time in Asia; for he was hurrying to be in Jerusalem, if possible, on the day of Pentecost. (Acts 20:16)

What's the hurry, Paul? And why Jerusalem? Why not stop at Ephesus where so much of your ministry has been accomplished? (Acts 19). It is likely that if Paul had stopped at Ephesus he would have been delayed by many old friends desiring to see him, and Paul was prioritizing to get to Jerusalem by Pentecost.

Three times a year all Jews everywhere were to come to Jerusalem and to the Temple for worship: The Feasts of Passover, Pentecost, and Tabernacles (Deuteronomy 16:16). Though people came to the Temple at Passover, there were more out of town Jews able to come to Jerusalem at Pentecost[9]. This was mainly because the favorable weather later in the spring made the roads passable, and Jerusalem more accessible.

That is why we read that multitudes were coming from different nations to Jerusalem at Pentecost. Messiah had promised His disciples that His Spirit would empower them to be His witnesses as they reached the world with the Good News (Acts 1:8). At that Pentecost, the Holy Spirit, was given to the body of believers in Yeshua. The many countries represented by individuals who received the pouring forth of the Spirit pictured God reaching out to the whole world.

9 see Josephus' Antiquities 14,13,4 and 17,10,2

101

This was Paul's priority: to make the most of every opportunity for the sake of the Good News. Hence he would write, "Walk in wisdom toward those who are outside, redeeming the time" (Ephesians 5:15-16).

Paul's priority reminds us of our ultimate purpose in life while on this side of heaven: to share Good News with those around us. Whether it is a feast day, a family event, work time or leisure, let us take every opportunity to share the love of God and reach out with the message of Messiah to all with ears to hear, even to the Jew first.

Pentecost is the last of the Spring Feasts, after which comes the summer of harvest. In God's timeline, we see that the Spring Feasts all deal with events that have come to fruition in the life of Yeshua and His early followers.

However, according to the Scriptures these appointed times point to "things to come" (Colossians 2:17). This point will come into focus as we look at the three appointed times occuring in the seventh month, rounding out our study of Leviticus 23.

QUESTIONS FOR SHAVUOT:

1. What did the Israelites do when Moses delayed coming
down from Mt Sinai? *made a golden calf*

2. How was the outpouring of the Spirit like the giving of
the Law and how was it different?

3. How is Shavuot "dateless"? What is "counting the
omer"? *obey God's "*

4. How is it significant that two loaves were required for
the Shavuot offering? *written + oral law*
humility + submission

5. What are the "two firstfruits"? How does there
symbolism relate? *barley, wheat, give your best to God*

6. Why was celebrating Pentecost a priority for Paul?
each male Jew had to attend

2. God gave us law + Holy Spirit
to Jews so they could go out + grow
Christ

the leaven - represents = sin also
Lev 23:18-20 bloody sin offering also grain
2 loaves, written + oral law -

103

GOD IS GATHERING
THE BODY OF MESSIAH

through

ראש השנה

ROSH HASHANAH

CHAPTER 5

THE FEAST OF TRUMPETS

ראש השנה

Our Gathering Unto The Lord

IN THE TORAH

> Speak to the sons of Israel, saying, "In the seventh
> month on the first of the month, you shall have a rest, a
> reminder by blowing of trumpets, a holy convocation.
> You shall not do any laborious work, but you shall
> present an offering by fire to the LORD." (Leviticus
> 23:24-25)

Growing up in Middle Village, Queens, NY, I can still
remember hearing the trumpeting of the High Holy Days
shofar that called us to assemble for worship. After coming
to faith in Messiah Yeshua, I was intrigued to see how the
shofar, or ram's horn, played such a significant role in
Scriptures. In fact, what is traditionally *Rosh Hashanah*,
or the Jewish New Year, is called in the Scriptures
Yom HaTeruah, which means "the Day of Blowing (by
Trumpets)."

The name Feast of Trumpets is not as well known since this feast is more commonly called Rosh Hashanah which we will cover later in this chapter. Jewish tradition purports that the blowing of trumpets is a reminder of the shofars (the shofar is made from a ram's horn) that Joshua and the Israelites used at Jericho, and also the horn of the ram that Abraham sacrificed in place of Isaac.

Scripture reveals even more about the prophetic meaning of the Feast of Trumpets. This feast points forward to a time when Israel will be gathered back to the land (Isaiah 27:13). Ultimately, it points to an instant when the Body of Messiah will be gathered, or "caught up" to meet the Lord (1 Corinthians 15:51-52; 1 Thessalonians 4:16-18).

FROM RAMS AND SILVER

There are actually two types of trumpets mentioned in the Bible: the silver trumpets, and the ram's horn. Their usage in the Scriptures tell a story all their own.

The silver trumpets in Numbers 10:2 hints at a reminder of our redemption before God, "Make yourself two trumpets of silver, of hammered work you shall make them; and you shall use them for summoning the congregation and for having the camps set out."

Why was silver used? It is likely that the silver was from the temple tax or the half shekel according to the sanctuary that all redeemed people had to pay to demonstrate that they are ransomed from bondage by the Lord:

> This is what everyone who is numbered shall give: half a shekel according to the shekel of the sanctuary (the

shekel is twenty gerahs), half a shekel as a contribution to the LORD. Everyone who is numbered, from twenty years old and over, shall give the contribution to the LORD. The rich shall not pay more and the poor shall not pay less than the half shekel, when you give the contribution to the LORD to make atonement for yourselves. (Exodus 30:13-16)

It is important to understand that no one could buy his own redemption; however, the half shekel was a memorial of his redemption.

GETTING CAUGHT UP

Trumpets were used in Scripture for many occasions and purposes:

- A call to assembly
- A command for Israel to move out
- A call to war
- Preparation for an announcement
- A warning of judgment to come
- A call to celebration and worship

Whenever these silver trumpets were blown either for assembly or alarm, for worship or for war, the redeemed of the Lord would respond.

The silver trumpets were used primarily in the Temple, so when the Temple was destroyed in AD 70, the use of the silver trumpets, along with much of the Temple paraphernalia, was discontinued. At that time the ram's horn took on a ubiquitous role in the feast. Because so little is said about this feast in the Hebrew Scriptures, there has always been a sense of mystery regarding what the

Feast of Trumpets refers to. The rabbis looked to Israel's past spiritual experiences for the answer. Some looked to Exodus 19:16, where trumpets announced God's descent on Mt. Sinai to give the Torah to Moses. Other rabbinical traditions teach the blowing of trumpets is a reminder of the *shofarot* blown by Joshua and the Israelites at Jericho (Joshua 6). Most importantly, the *shofar* is taken as a reminder of the ram that Abraham sacrificed in place of his son Isaac (Genesis 22).

Though these are reminders of God's wonderful works in the past, Scripture reveals much more about this mysterious Feast. For it does not merely point us to the past, but to the future.

Even as resurrection is a concept taught throughout the Scriptures (Daniel 12:2), there is an aspect of the resurrection heralded by the Feast of Trumpets. This mystery is known as "the Rapture." There are two portions of New Covenant Scripture that deal with this future event, and in both we see the trumpet involved:

> Behold, I tell you a mystery; we shall not all sleep, but we shall all be changed, in a moment, in the twinkling of an eye, at the last trumpet; for the trumpet will sound, and the dead will be raised imperishable, and we shall be changed... (1 Corinthians 15:51-52).

Paul also writes:

> For the Lord Himself will descend from heaven with a shout, with the voice of the archangel, and with the trumpet of God; and the dead in Messiah shall rise first. Then we who are alive and remain shall be caught up together with them in the clouds to

meet the Lord in the air, and thus we shall always be with the Lord. Therefore comfort one another with these words. (1 Thessalonians 4:16-18)

One day the trumpet of God will sound, and we should always be ready to respond. Its true that the doctrine of "the Rapture" (from *rapturo* used in the Latin translation of "caught up" in the passage above) is sometimes dismissed as a topic of science-fiction. Still, the event described has powerful significance for us today. It is presented as imminent, the next thing on God's agenda. And since no one knows the exact time of this future *shofar* blast, the Feast of Trumpets is meant to provoke us to readiness and service. We are "looking for the blessed hope and the appearing of the glory of our great God and Savior, Messiah Yeshua" (Titus 2:13). This expectation motivates lives of service before the Lord. As John writes in his first epistle:

Beloved, now we are children of God, and it has not appeared as yet what we shall be. We know that, when He appears, we shall be like Him, because we shall see Him just as He is. And everyone who has this hope fixed on Him purifies himself, just as He is pure. (1 John 3:2-3)

LET THE READER UNDERSTAND

The Trumpet of the Lord will not only be the call for believers to go and meet the Lord in the air, but that same Trumpet will be the catalyst for the last seven years of this present age, the period known as "the time of Jacob's trouble" (Jeremiah 30:7). It is this period that our Lord Yeshua referred to when He said:

For then there will be a great tribulation, such as has not occurred since the beginning of the world until now, nor ever shall. And unless those days had been cut short, no life would have been saved; but for the sake of the elect those days shall be cut short. (Matthew 24:21-22)

It is difficult to imagine the sheer terror that people who are left will experience just at this time. Suddenly, without any apparent warning, millions of people will disappear from Planet Earth. In mid-sentence, mid-stride, loved ones, children, spouses, friends, co-workers all simply vanish. On a societal and governmental level, chaos will ensue.

Into this resulting void, the Scriptures warn, the ultimate false-messiah, the Anti-Christ, shall arise.

Let no one in any way deceive you, for it will not come unless the apostasy comes first, and the man of lawlessness is revealed, the son of destruction, who opposes and exalts himself above every so-called god or object of worship, so that he takes his seat in the temple of God, displaying himself as being God. (2 Thessalonians 2:3-4)

This false Messiah will not oppose God overtly, but subtly, just as the serpent opposed the truth and deceived Eve in the Garden of Eden. The man of sin will claim to be the true messiah, by promising peace he will deceive the world. As Daniel writes, he will "by peace destroy many," leading this world in rebellion against God, down the road to sudden destruction (Daniel 8:25).

This false savior will go into the yet-to-be-rebuilt temple in Jerusalem, declare Himself to be God, and then declare all-out war against Israel. Regarding this, Yeshua said:

> Therefore when you see the abomination of desolation which was spoken of through Daniel the prophet, standing in the holy place (let the reader understand), then let those who are in Judea flee to the mountains. (Matthew 24:15-16)

The day is coming when man must reckon with his Maker. In God's great love and patience He bears long with us, "not willing that any should perish, but that all should come to repentance" (2 Peter. 3:9). God does, however, allow circumstances to get to a point in our lives where we have nowhere else to turn, but to Him. This will be Israel's situation in the time yet to come (Joel 2:1-2, 12-15).

For followers of Messiah, the hope for Israel is not only that they to return to the land, but also to the Lord. May we reach out to people today, and seek to lead them to Messiah while there is time, to believe now, before the day of wrath appears.

Yeshua said that we "must work the works of Him who sent Me, as long as it is day; night is coming, when no man can work" (John 9:4). Redeeming the time, let us re-evaluate our lives, priorities, and schedules, as we care for those around us. The Good News of Messiah is for Jews and Gentiles alike, as we wait expectantly for the Feast of Trumpets, and our Messiah's glorious return.

THE JEWISH NEW YEAR

Again, the Feast of Trumpets is more commonly called Rosh Hashanah[10], or the Jewish New Year which falls on the lunar month of Tishri (September-October). How did we come up with the New Year in the seventh month? As one of four traditional "new years," the idea might well have developed when the Jewish people came out of the Babylonian captivity, wherein we adopted the Babylonian civil New Year as our own (Tishri is actually a Babylonian word meaning "beginning.").

Over the centuries, tradition accepted it as one of four new years, and the rabbis developed various explanations surrounding the day. Rosh Hashanah became the most prominent, especially because, according to tradition, humanity was created on this day[11].

TRADITIONS WITH MEANING

Rosh Hashanah introduces the most serious season in the Jewish calendar know as *Yamin Noraim*, the Days of Awe. This period includes ten days of introspection and repentance, leading to Yom Kippur on the tenth day. It is a time of soul searching and of making things right with God and one's neighbors.

Today Jewish people celebrate Rosh Hashanah through various traditions. One of the traditions is partaking of foods such as honey cake and apples dipped in honey, which symbolize our peoples' hope for a sweet and happy new year. We greet one another at this time of year with

---

[10] Rosh Hashanah means "the head of the year"

[11] B. Talmud, Rosh Hashanah 1a, 8a-18a

the traditional phrase, "May you be inscribed [in the Book of Life] for a good year!" (*L'shana tovah tikatayvu*).

The synagogue service during *Rosh Hashanah* includes three fundamental sections. The first section is called *Malkiyot* (Kingships) emphasizing the fact of God's sovereignty. The second section is called *Zikhronot* (Remembrance) which testifies to the fact that our God is a God who remembers His covenants and promises to Israel. The third section is the *Shofarot* section when the shofar is blown. The shofar brings to memory God's provision of the ram that Abraham sacrificed in place of his only son, Isaac, and we have seen from the Scriptures that the shofar has more of a prophetic meaning.

Additionally, some observe *Tashlich*, a tradition which began in the fifteenth century is still practiced today. From a Hebrew word meaning "to cast," *Tashlich* involves going to the sea shore or to the bank of a river on the afternoon of the first day of Rosh Hashanah. At the water's edge, participants toss bread crumbs into the water as prayers are said regarding God's forgiveness. This recalls the words of the prophet Micah:

> He will again have compassion on us; He will tread our iniquities underfoot. Yes, You will cast all their sins into the depths of the sea. (Micah 7:19)

A NEW HEART FOR A NEW LIFE

The Scriptures, however, require more than ritual to be forgiven by God. In the end, as meaningful as tradition is, a New Year celebration may only update last year's problems and pain.

The Bible teaches that the Lord will give the free gift of new life at any time to all who will come to Him. God says that Israel will nationally receive this new life when they look upon "Me whom they have pierced" (Zechariah 12:10). But individually we may receive this new life now by faith in Him. The prophet Ezekiel reveals the gift of new life that God wants us to have.

> "Then I will sprinkle clean water on you [Israel], and you will be clean; I will cleanse you from all your filthiness and from all your idols. And, I will give you a new heart and put a new spirit within you; and I will remove the heart of stone from your flesh and give you a heart of flesh. I will put My Spirit within you and cause you to walk in My statutes, and you will be careful to observe My ordinances." (Ezekiel 36:25-27)

It is estimated that ninety three percent of recorded human history is comprised of warfare. What is wrong with us? To simply say, "I'm OK, you're OK," or "you have your own view of reality, and I have mine," or "let's accentuate the positive" is simply an attempt to avoid the desperate, wretched condition of the human heart.

All of history abundantly testifies to our sad condition– and where it is taking us. Something is definitely wrong with us humans and that something is sin. The fact is our hearts were corrupted when Adam fell (Genesis 3). We have left a trail of broken promises, broken hearts, and broken lives down through the ages. The prophet Isaiah testifies to our heart condition:

> For all of us have become like one who is unclean, and
> all our righteous deeds are like a filthy garment; and

all of us wither like a leaf, and our iniquities, like the wind, take us away. (Isaiah 64:6)

For example, if one person has a crippling disease we are concerned; but if all of us have that same crippling disease then it becomes a plague; we are compelled to find a solution. The need is revealed throughout the Scriptures. Through David's psalm of repentance we read:

Purify me with hyssop, and I shall be clean; Wash me, and I shall be whiter than snow. Wash me thoroughly from my iniquity and cleanse me from my sin. (Psalm 51:2, 7)

God has provided a cure. Notice in each case the basis is what God can do, provided we are willing to receive His cure. "If we confess our sins, He is faithful and righteous to forgive us our sins and to cleanse us from all unrighteousness" (1 John 1:9).

Traditionally Rosh Hashanah is seen as the time of hope when your name could be written in the "Book of Life" for the coming year. But, the Bible teaches that the Lord is desirous to inscribe your name in the Lamb's book of life (Revelation 20) not just for a year, but for eternity. God offers new life to all who will come to Him. Just as we personally receive new life now by faith in Yeshua, so also one day Israel as a nation will be restored to God.

These days, the issue of purity is open to public derision. The Hebrew word for "filthiness" is *tum'ah,* and means uncleanness. It also refers to unclean spirits, which among other things, inspired false prophets to lie.

When it says, "I will sprinkle clean water on you," it refers to ceremonial cleansing that recognizes God's forgiveness. In Isaiah 52:15 it says, "Thus He will sprinkle many nations, kings will shut their mouths on account of Him; for what had not been told them they will see, and what they had not heard they will understand." Messiah is the One who is applying His atonement as He sprinkles many nations. In the New Covenant we see how this very sprinkling was fulfilled for each person who trusts in Yeshua.

> Let us draw near with a sincere heart in full assurance of faith, having our hearts sprinkled clean from an evil conscience and our bodies washed with pure water. (Hebrews 10:22)

This is why the Lord promised through Ezekiel "I will give you a [new] heart of flesh." In this context "heart" refers to a person's nature. A hard-hearted person is insensitive to others, and to God. A tenderhearted person will be sensitive to God's concerns, and care for those around him. Ruach HaKodesh (the Holy Spirit) will empower your life and keep you sensitive to the things which matter most to Him. The New Covenant declares that the Spirit of the Living God is available to all who will believe in Messiah, as seen when a Pharisee named Nicodemus came to Yeshua.

> "Rabbi, we know that You have come from God as a teacher; for no one can do these signs that You do unless God is with him."
>
> Yeshua answered, "unless one is born again he cannot see the kingdom of God."
>
> "How can a man be born when he is old? He cannot enter a second time into his mother's womb and be born, can he?"

"Truly, truly, I say to you, unless one is born of water and the Spirit he cannot enter into the kingdom of God" (John 3:3-5)

The picture of clean water cleansing our moral filth and sins illustrates the true cleansing agent of God which alone can atone for sins: the blood of Messiah.

Draw near to God and He will draw near to you. Cleanse your hands, you sinners; and purify your hearts, you double-minded. (James 4:8)

There is a kind who is pure in his own eyes, yet is not washed from his filthiness. (Proverbs 30:12)

For the life of the flesh is in the blood, and I have given it to you upon the altar to make atonement for your souls; for it is the blood that makes atonement for the soul. (Leviticus 17:11)

Animal sacrifices in the *Tanakh* were insufficient for totally removing and cleansing sin permanently, hence they were repeated year after year. But the writer of Hebrews tells us,

How much more will the blood of Messiah, who through the eternal Spirit offered Himself without blemish to God, cleanse your conscience from dead works to serve the living God? (Hebrews 9:14)

To illustrate the need to replace our defective hearts there is a story about pacemakers. In the late 70s General Electric recalled 487 pacemakers because of a defective part. It meant inconvenience to many and a costly bill to GE. In a similar way God is putting out a universal recall to all heart recipients: a new heart for the old, defective, and heart of stone that is presently within you. A defective heart will cause eternal misery unless replaced!

In this context "the heart" refers to a person's nature. A stony or hard-hearted person is insensitive to others, to God, and His will. A tenderhearted person will be sensitive to God's concerns, and will care for those around him. If we do not share God's passion and concerns, we will not share the joy of His victories? Life sometimes throws situations at us we do not always appreciate, or even like.

God does not promise to change your circumstances, but He will change your heart amidst the circumstances. The heart of flesh that God gives is able to bring encouragement, even though our circumstances may appear troublesome.

One young man in college, a believer in Messiah, had to permanently use crutches to get around. Though considered handicapped, he seemed so happy, and was always busy helping others. One day a curious student asked him why he had to use crutches. The believer simply answered, "Infantile paralysis."

The student asked, "How can you bear to go on and help others with such joy?"

"Oh," the believer replied, "The disease never touched my heart."

God can enable you by His Holy Spirit to live a triumphal life despite the difficulties. God's Spirit of life, the Holy Spirit (*Ruach HaKodesh*) will empower your life and keep you sensitive to His will. The New Covenant declares that the Spirit of the Living God is available to all who will believe in Messiah.

This is the word of the LORD to Zerubbabel saying, "Not by might nor by power, but by My Spirit," says the LORD of hosts. (Zechariah 4:6)

But if the Spirit of Him who raised Yeshua from the dead dwells in you, He who raised Messiah Yeshua from the dead will also give life to your mortal bodies through His Spirit who dwells in you. (Romans 8:11)

That He would grant you, according to the riches of His glory, to be strengthened with power through His Spirit in the inner person. (Ephesians 3:16)

The purpose of the Holy Spirit (*Ruach HaKodesh*) living in us is that He may live His life through us: that we may live like Him, and love like Him. It is through obedience that we demonstrate that God's Word is true. Such trust, or faith, allows God to turn obstacles into opportunities. His Spirit enables you and me to live the life He called us to live. God can help you live a life worth living. His transforming power is not only able to change our situations, but to change us in our situations, that His grace might prove all-sufficient for our lives (Galatians 5:22-23). God not only wants us to be with Him, but to be like Him. Our new resource enables us to live new and different lives. Messiah came to bring new life for a new year!

QUESTIONS FOR THE FEAST OF TRUMPETS:

1. What ever happened to the silver trumpets? *in Bobylin*
   & from temple has gone after 70 AD
2. What future event does this feast symbolize, and
   where is that event found in the Scriptures?
   I Coron 15:51-52   I Thes 4:16-18
3. How might have this feast come to be called Rosh
   HaShanah (the Jewish New Year)?

4. What are the main elements of a Rosh HaShanah *p.114*
   service in the synagogue today? What is *tashlich*?
   worship
5. How does the Bible teach that our sins may be *bread onto*
   forgiven? *Jesus*   *water*

6. How did Yeshua fulfill the phrase "I will sprinkle
   clean water on you" from Ezekiel 36:25-27?

1 Kingship - God's sovereignty
2 remembrance - God remembers His covenants,
   promises to Israel
3 shofars blown - mercy of God - provision
   of ram to Abraham for Issac
Some cast bread on water
   cast sins into sea p. 114
   Micah 7:19

hope that God puts your name
   in Book of Life

121

69
atonement one of sin
concerning
reconciliation of Sin
twix God & humanity

Ten Days Awe
Tens of Repentance

Lev 16:1-34, 23:26-32

76 What is main focus of Day of Atonement

Why do we need blood atonement for sin

p 74 4. humbling

p 77: priest Aron - Levi
1
2
3
4   Copy p. 78

p 78   Copy Tabernacle
11

GOD IS GATHERING
HIS PEOPLE ISRAEL

through

יום כפור

YOM KIPPUR

CHAPTER 6

THE DAY OF ATONEMENT

יום כפור

ONE SACRIFICE FOR ALL TIME

IN THE TORAH

The LORD spoke to Moses, saying: "On exactly the tenth day of this seventh month is the Day of Atonement; it shall be a holy convocation for you, and you shall humble your souls and present an offering by fire to the LORD. You shall not do any work on this same day, for it is a day of atonement, to make atonement on your behalf before the LORD your God. If there is any person who will not humble himself on this same day, he shall be cut off from his people. As for any person who does any work on this same day, that person I will destroy from among his people. You shall do no work at all. It is to be a perpetual statute throughout your generations in all your dwelling places. It is to be a sabbath of complete rest to you, and you shall humble your souls; on the ninth of the month at evening, from evening until evening, you shall keep your sabbath." (Leviticus 23:26-32)

OVERVIEW

Each year Jewish people observe Yom Kippur (the Day of Atonement) as the holiest day of the year, by reviewing their lives before God. Although Yom Kippur is an opportunity for individual restoration to God, in the portion above, the Hebrew verbs and pronouns are in the plural form ("you shall humble your souls"). Each year, the Day of Atonement was the day for the nation of Israel as a whole to be restored as a holy people to the Lord.

Today, because of national unbelief, Israel has been sidetracked from the fullness of its service. Nevertheless, the time will come for Israel to be gathered back to God as a nation. During the Tribulation, Israel will be brought back to the forefront of service. At the end of that Tribulation period, a nation shall be born in a day, and "thus all Israel will be saved" (Romans 11:26).

LIFE AND DEATH

Rosh Hashanah and Yom Kippur are referred to as the High Holy Days. They are days of solemn personal evaluation of one's soul before God. In the traditional Jewish community, Rosh Hashanah is seen as the Day of Judgment: when God evaluates an individual's deeds to determine whether He will write that person's name in the Book of Life for the coming year[12].

---

[12] Talmud, Rosh Hashanah 16a

According to tradition, on Rosh Hashanah three books are opened before God in Heaven. One book is for the absolutely wicked. Their names will not be written in the "Book of Life" for the coming year. Another book is for the perfectly righteous. Their names will be written in the Book of Life for the coming year (I imagine this is not a very big book!). Finally, the third book is opened for those not in either of the first two books, those ordinary people who are neither perfectly evil nor perfectly good.

After the books are opened on Rosh Hashanah, people then have ten days to do good deeds to merit being placed in the Book of Life for the coming year. These ten days are called "the Days of Awe" and they end at Yom Kippur. On Yom Kippur, people return to synagogue in order to repent of their sins with the hope that they have been forgiven by God and that their names have been written into the Book of Life for the coming year.

Therefore, to be made right with God is the desire of every religious Jew on Yom Kippur (and on Yom Kippur, we also become a bit more religious). It is believed that repentance with fasting, charity, and good deeds produce forgiveness. Though fasting on Yom Kippur is not the specific scriptural command, the day is so commonly identified with the practice that it is even called "the fast" in the New Covenant (Acts 27:9) Biblically, Yom Kippur was the day God set apart to restore relationship between Himself and His people.

It is called a "holy convocation" (Leviticus 23:27), literally a "holy calling" for the nation. Other than fasting for a day, the need for an actual, physical sacrifice is not recognized by most Jewish people today. The concept of a vicarious blood sacrifice is considered archaic by most people, including traditional Judaism.

Some rabbis contend that the Bible provides atonement without a bloody sacrifice, even in biblical times. At any rate, with the destruction of the Temple by the Romans in AD 70, there has been no acceptable place for blood sacrifice. Thus, the rabbis have concluded from this that God no longer required blood sacrifice for the forgiveness of sins. However, what does Scripture say say on the subject? The texts are clear:

> For the life of the flesh is in the blood, and I have given it to you on the altar to make atonement for your souls; for it is the blood by reason of the life that makes atonement.[13]

The blood, representing life, makes atonement for the soul. It has been thought that there were bloodless sacrifices made, such as the flour offering for the poor. Therefore, it is argued, God would accept bloodless sacrifices, and must accept us without bloody sacrifice as well. Leviticus shows this premise not to be so:

> But if his means are insufficient for two turtledoves or two young pigeons, then for his offering for that which he has sinned, he shall bring the tenth of an ephah of fine flour for a sin offering; he shall not put oil on it or place incense on it, for it is a sin offering. He shall bring it to the priest, and the priest shall take his handful of

---

[13] Leviticus 17:11, and 16:2-34 for special sacrifices for Yom Kippur atonement.

it as its memorial portion and offer it up in smoke on the altar, with the offerings of the LORD by fire: it is a sin offering. (Leviticus 5:11-12)

When we look carefully at the text, we see that the flour was only acceptable when laid upon and identified with the bloody offerings, "And offer it up in smoke on the altar, with [on top of, or upon] the offerings of the LORD by fire: it is a sin offering" (Leviticus 5:12). When the flour offering was laid upon the bloody sacrifice, in so doing it became bloody itself. There was never a sacrifice that expiated sin that was not bloody.

TOWARD THE HOUSE

In another era of history, we Jewish people found ourselves captive in Babylon, outside our homeland of Israel. To make things worse, there no longer was a Temple where we could make sacrifices, since the armies of Nebuchadnezzar had destroyed it. One man who found himself in Babylon was Daniel. Since Daniel was unable to make sacrifice but yet was forgiven, it is assumed that we also can be forgiven without sacrifice. However, it is a false assumption that Daniel did not trust in the blood sacrifice of the Temple, the house of God.

Did you ever wonder why Daniel prayed three times a day with his face towards Jerusalem, despite the danger in doing so? Daniel's godly lifestyle agitated his contemporaries, and because they envied his success, they conspired to get rid of him. "Now when Daniel knew that the document was signed [for his condemnation], he entered his house (now in his roof chamber he had windows open toward Jerusalem); and he continued kneeling on his knees three times a day, praying and giving thanks before his God, as he had been doing previously" (Daniel 6:10). To understand the need to pray toward Jerusalem more fully, please note Solomon's prayer when he consecrated the Temple in Jerusalem:

> When they (Israel) sin against You (for there is no man who does not sin) and You are angry with them and deliver them to an enemy, so that they take them away captive to the land of the enemy, far off or near; if they take thought in the land where they have been taken captive, and repent and make supplication to You in the land of those who have taken them captive, saying, "We have sinned and have committed iniquity, we have acted wickedly;" if they return to You with all their heart and with all their soul in the land of their enemies who have taken them captive, and pray to You toward their land which You have given to their fathers, the city which You have chosen, and the house (the temple) which I have built for Your name; then hear their prayer and their supplication in heaven Your dwelling place. (1 Kings 8:46-49)

In this portion of Scripture, Solomon asks God to hear the prayers of His people even when they are in exile due to sin.

Solomon pleads to God to forgive their sins when they pray toward the House of the Lord. That is why when Daniel was in exile he had confidence to pray toward Solomon's Temple in Jerusalem, the place of blood sacrifice. Daniel identified with the sacrifices and found forgiveness. This is why even today synagogues are built facing Jerusalem and the Temple area, though the Temple is no longer standing. Now that the substance is here, Yeshua, to which sacrificial system and Temple points, we pray from wherever we are in His name. He is the sacrifice we look to, identify with, and depend on.

One might wonder, "doesn't a substitutionary sacrifice demean a person's responsibility to account for their own offences?" The biblical fact of substitutionary atonement has never removed the personal responsibility of the offender, and restitution to the offended party. However, the reality is that sin against God is so heinous and costly that no personal sacrifice can satisfactorily pay for the offence. Just because you can break a Ming vase, does not mean you can afford to pay for it!

We were created to live lives of praise to God, depending on Him. For this, we are responsible. But this does not diminish the weight of sin and the need for sacrifice. Has God changed His view of sacrifice, or have we merely changed our view of sin? Perhaps people have accepted an idea of sin as a minor infraction, where a day of fasting is seen as sufficient to get right with God. However, is this acceptable to God, the offended party? He states that sin is catastrophic to His honor, our well-being, and our relationships. Since His view on sin has not changed, our view on sacrifice should not either.

Blood, so obviously necessary to life, plays the major role in the sacrificial system, and did so from the time of the sacrifice by Abel (Genesis 4:4). God told Noah that man's blood was sacred, for it represents the life of man created in God's image (Genesis 9:6). Also, that the people were forbidden to eat animal blood further emphasizes this fact (Leviticus 17:14). By rejecting blood atonement the rabbis both demeaned the holiness of God and minimized the offensiveness of sin. To offend an Eternal God's holiness is an eternal offense, and therefore requires an atonement of life.

Thus, while this topic of blood can seem bizarre or primitive, the sacrifices are meant to teach us the real horror of sin: sin kills.

A RESTORED RELATIONSHIP

Biblical Jewish faith takes *teshuvah* (repentance) along with blood sacrifice as both essential for atonement.

Our calling as a people is to humble ourselves, because only the sacrifice makes us acceptable before God. The word *kippur* in Hebrew means to cover, and refers to an atonement by vicarious, substitutionary methods. Blood atonement is the basis for our restored relationship with God. In Leviticus 23:26-32, we have atonement principles that provide a promise of certain restoration with God.

At the end of verse 27 of Leviticus 23 we find the phrase, "You shall offer an offering made by fire unto the LORD." Not only was the offering to be made by fire unto the Lord, furthermore it had to be a bloody offering according to Leviticus 17:11, "For the life of the flesh is in the blood...for it is the blood that maketh an atonement for the soul." The burnt offering pictures a total consuming of the worshiper before God. The shedding of the blood of an innocent animal shows how serious our sinful offenses are toward a Holy God. Real relationships require real sacrifice. Atonement by blood is necessary because of sin's effect. God wants your passion, not just your ashes.

In the Hebrew Scriptures, blood sacrifice was assumed, as the sacrifices of that day were detailed out in Leviticus 16 and Numbers 29:7-11. Regarding Leviticus 23 and the Day of Atonement portion, only a brief allusion is made to the sacrifice; instead, the text emphasizes humility. Yom Kippur is about God reconciling Himself to His Covenant people. Even though we are the offenders, God took the initiative to restore a relationship with us. He provided all that is needed in Messiah.

> You shall humble your souls and present an offering by fire to the Lord... Because (If there is) any person who will not humble himself on this same day, he shall be cut off from his people. (Leviticus 23:27, 29)

The Scripture says, "You shall humble your souls." Humility involves our mind, emotions, and will. As a love relationship involves submitting oneself to the concerns of the other person, out of concern for that person, even so Messiah submitted Himself to die for us all. Because of His love for us, Messiah demonstrates humility by counting our welfare more important than His own dignity.

We demonstrate humility when we accept the atonement of God by faith. Atonement was based on the offerings that were made for the cleansing of sins (Leviticus 16), but without humility those offerings would have been in vain. It is through humility that we can relate to God and understand that our lives need to be God-oriented, not self-oriented. God provides His rest so we can cease from self-oriented activities and works. Yom Kippur reminds us that we are fallen creatures resting only in the grace, mercy, and atonement of God in Messiah. Works apart from Messiah are self-oriented activities which are mere efforts to prove what we can do. Biblical humility is essential to restoring relationships. Only through this humility we can apply and enjoy the benefits of forgiveness in the atonement made in Messiah. Here are five simple steps to reconciliation now, and forever.

1. CONFESSION: RECOGNITION OF OUR SINS

As we have seen, sin breaks a relationship when we care for ourselves rather than for others. Recognize and identify with the offense you caused. Do not blame others or look at others perceived shortcomings, but take responsibility for your own actions and attitudes. Admit wrongdoing; confess it as a wrong, not just a mistake. Negligence and unawareness for others is indifference, self-preoccupation and a lack of love. Admit your wrongs in all humility and honesty.

2. CONTRITION: REMORSE OVER OUR SINS

Realize the offense you caused and identify with that offense, as if it happened to you. That will produce remorse and empathy with the offended party. Do not minimize the offense to others simply because you are insensitive or unconcerned about those same offenses. Breaking your wife's high heel because you used it to swat a fly may not break your heart, but imagine if someone broke your electric power saw doing the same thing.

> For I know my transgressions, and my sin is ever before me. Against You, You only, I have sinned and done what is evil in Your sight, So that You are justified when You speak And blameless when You judge. (Psalm 51:3-4)

3. CONVERSION: REPENTANCE FROM OUR SINS

Humility does not mock repentance. To repent is to turn away from an improper attitude or action. For example, if you blow up at your spouse, do not attempt to justify your offense by saying, "Oh, I'm just an angry sort of person." This justifies nothing. We must deal with sin as sin. Unconfessed sin hurts you by both undermining your integrity, and hardening your heart to the people around you. As David learned, many are "sin-sick" from unconfessed, unrepented sin.

> When I kept silent about my sin, my body wasted away through my groaning all day long. For day and night Your hand was heavy upon me; My vitality was drained away as with the fever heat of summer. I acknowledged my sin to You, and my iniquity I did not hide; I said, "I will confess my transgressions to the LORD"; And You forgave the guilt of my sin. (Psalm 32:3-5)

4. COMPENSATION: REPAYMENT FOR OUR SINS

Because it would take all eternity, we could never pay for our own sins. Therefore, Messiah chose to die as payment for our sins. This, however, does not negate our responsibility to pay our debts to our fellow man. True humility repays when possible. Like Zacchaeus in the New Covenant, this demonstrates sincerity of faith with a humble attitude of trust in Messiah.

> And Zacchaeus stood, and said unto the Lord; Behold, Lord, the half of my goods I give to the poor; and if I have taken any thing from any man by false accusation, I restore him fourfold. And Jesus said unto him, this day is salvation come to this house, forasmuch as he also is a son of Abraham. (Luke 19:8-9)

When my friend Stewart came to faith in Messiah, he then went and repaid each person he stole from before he accepted Yeshua. Why? God's grace is not an excuse for irresponsibility. God's grace provides the opportunity and the enablement to honor Yeshua in all our ways.

5. CONSECRATION: DEDICATION BEYOND OUR SINS

True humility is seen in making lifestyle changes that reflect true love, and a love for the truth. The standard by which we are called to live is given to us by Messiah Himself, "love the lord your God with all your heart and soul and might" and "love your neighbor as your self" (Mark 12:29-31).

In Ephesians 4:24-28 we learn that if we depend upon God's grace, His Spirit will enable us:

- To change: "And put on the new self, which in the likeness of God has been created in righteousness and holiness of the truth."

- To be honest: "Therefore, laying aside falsehood, speak truth every one with his neighbor for we are members of one another."

- To exercise self-control: "Be angry and yet do not sin; do not let the sun go down on your anger."

- To obtain victory over our adversary: "And do not give the devil an opportunity."

- To live a honorable, productive life: "He who steals must steal no longer; but rather he must labor, performing with his own hands what is good, so that he will have something to share with one who has need."

The blessing in life is not merely knowing what to do, but in actually doing it. "If you know these things blessed are you that do them" (John 13:17). Who is most humble? Well, it is not a contest. However, the one who wants to reconcile the most will sacrifice the most to do it. God has demonstrated true humility through Messiah. It was prophesied that when King Messiah would come we would see the humility of God manifested:

> Rejoice greatly, O daughter of Zion! Shout, O daughter of Jerusalem! Behold, your King is coming to you; He is just and having salvation, humble and riding on a donkey, a colt, the foal of a donkey. (Zechariah 9:9)

So when Yeshua invited people to trust in Him it was because of His humility and genuine concern for them.

> Come to Me, all who are weary and heavy-laden, and I will give you rest. Take My yoke upon you and learn from Me, for I am gentle and humble in heart, and You will find rest for your souls. For My yoke is easy and My burden is light. (Matthew 11:28-30)

An attitude of humility is the safest position for sinners to be in: if you lie on the ground you can not fall down. When Messiah's atonement is applied to your life, humility is manifested in your marriage, business, and other relationships. This way God gets all the glory. Genuine repentance and humility of soul is the basis for relating to one another, especially to God. This section from the New Covenant speaks to this vital issue:

> Let nothing be done through selfish ambition or conceit, but in lowliness of mind let each esteem

others better than himself. Let each of you look out not only for his own interests, but also for the interests of others. Let this mind be in you which was also in Messiah Yeshua, who, being in the form of God, did not consider it robbery to be equal with God, but made Himself of no reputation, taking the form of a bondservant, and coming in the likeness of men. And being found in appearance as a man, He humbled Himself and became obedient to the point of death, even the death of the cross. (Philippians 2:3-8)

This is the key to success in relating to others. Even as Yeshua, the Humble King, came and died that we might live, we are to seek their good rather than our own. Your acquaintances will likely want to be your friends, if you humbly put others ahead of yourself.

Do you want your life to be spiritually fulfilled? God can bring contentment to your soul, and actually wants your life fulfilled more than you do. Recognize that only God can fulfill your life.

THE BELIEVER'S REST

It shall be unto you a sabbath of rest, and ye shall afflict your souls: in the ninth day of the month at even, from even unto even, shall ye celebrate your sabbath. (Leviticus 23:30)

We recall from chapter 1 that the root Hebrew word for Shabbat is *yashav*, meaning to rest, or to sit down. Relationship is a resting together, not just working together. In a marriage this is illustrated by the problem of an empty nest syndrome. Once the kids are raised and gone, the marriage relationship may seem to lose meaning and purpose. The work and activities that once occupied the couple's time have changed. Suddenly the couple finds themselves with empty lives. Having a sacrifice may pay for offenses committed, and the humbling of the soul may speak of the sincere sorrow for those sins, but that still does not mean that we actually resting with the Lord. Beyond sacrifices and humility, God desires relationship.

Shabbat means resting in time: taking the time to pray, or talk with God; time to read Scripture, or hear from God. It is a time not to look to your performance or productivity as the meaning of your life, but to look to God and His gracious character.

Messiah came that we might have abundant spiritual life, not an abundance of materialistic clutter. Rest is a time to enjoy, learn, and grow in friendship with God, which is the very reason you are alive.

LOOKING UNTO YESHUA

When we pray "looking unto Yeshua the author and finisher of our faith" (Hebrews 12:2), we identify with the final blood sacrifice that was made for our atonement. Thus, we find forgiveness for our sins. Just as Daniel had to look to the Temple, we must realize, One has come, who is "greater than the Temple" (Matthew 12:6). For Messiah has come and has made final and effective atonement for all who will believe. All the sacrifices of bulls and goats could not remove sins, but only temporarily cover over sins. Those sacrifices were pointing to Messiah Yeshua, the true, effective and eternal sacrifice for all our sins. Thus, the New Covenant says:

> For the law...can never with these same sacrifices, which they offer continually year by year, make those who approach perfect...For it is not possible that the blood of bulls and goats could take away sins.... We have been sanctified through the offering of the body of Yeshua the Messiah once for all...For by one offering He has perfected forever those who are being sanctified. (Hebrews 10:1-14)

The principle of blood atonement found in the sacrificial system is not to be explained away. Rather, the sacrifices functioned like promissory notes which were paid off by Yeshua. Often the relationship between the sacrifices and Yeshua is misunderstood, as when it is objected that Yeshua could not have made atonement because He did not meet the requirements for the various sacrifices under the Mosaic law (He is not an animal, nor is He a grain, etc.). The reality is that all of the pieces are meant to point to One Who is far greater than the symbols themselves.

It would be wrong to conclude from the destruction of the Temple that blood atonement for forgiveness of sins is no longer required by God. Rather, the Messiah of Israel has come and made final and eternal atonement. That is why Yeshua declared from the cross, "It is finished" (John 19:30). God wants restored relationships between Him and His people. For that, there has to be redemption by blood, repentance by the believer and rest in the Beloved. Do you have this? If not, come to Yeshua, our sacrifice.

God's redemption is not to provide a great religion for His people, but to provide a great relationship with His people. It is not by good deeds during the Days of Awe that will gain entrance into the Book of Life, but by faith in God's finished work of atonement in Messiah. As we have seen, under pain of death our own works were not allowed on the Day of Atonement. Paul reiterates this idea in his letter to the congregation at Ephesus where he writes, "For by grace you have been saved through faith, and that not of yourselves; it is the gift of God, not of works, lest anyone should boast" (Ephesians 2:8-9).

Having trusted in God's Word regarding sin, atonement, and Messiah, you can "...rejoice that your names are recorded in heaven" (Luke 10:20). By faith in Yeshua as God's final atoning sacrifice, the New Year greeting– "*L'shana tova tikatevu*," or "May you be inscribed (in the Book of Life) for a good year"– can be fulfilled in your life. May your name be in this book of life "written from the foundation of the world in the book of life of the Lamb who has been slain" (Revelation 13:8).

YOM KIPPUR'S PROPHETIC SIGNIFICANCE

Yom Kippur is a day for Israel to be restored to God as a nation, when they trust in the Messiah (Leviticus 16, 23:26-32; Zechariah 12-14). This will come about through the tribulation period, which is called, in Jeremiah 30:7, "the time of Jacob's trouble." Anti-Semitism will reach its zenith, as all the nations of the world come against Israel, in an attempt to once and for all destroy the Jews. It is this time that will prepare Israel for the coming King Messiah and His kingdom. During the Tribulation period or the time of Jacob's trouble, Israel will be brought back to the forefront of service through the ministry of 144,000 Jewish evangelists. These evangelists will go forth to share the message of Messiah to prepare for the King's return and the establishment of His Kingdom.

> We have sealed the servants of our God on their foreheads. And I heard the number of those who were sealed. One hundred and forty-four thousand of all the tribes of the children of Israel were sealed: of the tribe of Judah twelve thousand were sealed... of the tribe of Reuben, ...Gad, ...Asher, ...Naphtali, ...Manasseh, ...Simeon, ...Levi, ...Issachar, ...Zebulon, ...Joseph, ...Benjamin twelve thousand were sealed." (Revelation 7:3-8)

At the end of the Tribulation period, the armies of the nations of the world will be gathered together to destroy Israel, and incredibly, to fight against Messiah. Armageddon is a term familiar to moviegoers, science fiction fans, and prophecy buffs, and it is found in the final book of Scripture.

> For they are spirits of demons, performing signs, which go out to the kings of the earth and of the whole world, to gather them to the battle of that great day of God Almighty. ...And they gathered them together to the place called in Hebrew, Armageddon (Revelation 16:14, 16).

> These will make war with the Lamb, and the Lamb will overcome them, for He is Lord of lords and King of kings; and those who are with Him are called, chosen, and faithful. (Revelation 17:14)

It is tragic, almost beyond belief, yet the Prophets declare that two-thirds of the Jewish people will be killed during this terrible time (Zechariah 13:8). Six million Jewish people were murdered during the Nazis' reign of terror, yet the worst is still to come. Today, we hear voices of anti-Semites chanting "Death to Israel" across the world. It is not hard to imagine that in the future, the declarations of Israel's enemies will seem to be on the verge of fulfillment: "They have said, 'Come, and let us cut them off from being a nation, that the name of Israel may be remembered no more'" (Psalm 83:4).

With the nations of the world hostile or indifferent, Israel will have nowhere else to turn. On the verge of slaughter and annihilation, she will cry out to her God in truth. At this point, Messiah will make His long awaited entrance to rescue His people. Messiah's heart-broken words will be fulfilled: "For I say to you, you shall see Me no more till you say, 'Blessed is He who comes in the name of the LORD'" (Matthew 23:39; Psalm 118:26).

THE GLORIOUS FUTURE OF ISRAEL

The Jewish people will recognize their Messiah as it is written:

- *In that day*, "...they shall look on Me [Messiah], the One they have pierced, and mourn for Him as one mourns for a firstborn son" (Zechariah 12:10).

- *In that day*, Israel will receive "cleansing from sin and impurity" (Zechariah 13:1).

- In *that day*, "...the stone which the builders rejected shall become the chief cornerstone" (Psalm 118:22).

- *In that day*, the great confession of Israel will be lamented, "All we like sheep have gone astray, each one has turned to his own way, but the LORD has laid on Him (Messiah) the iniquity of us all" (Isaiah 53:6).

Messiah will fight for Israel and rescue His people, and destroy her enemies:

> Now I saw heaven opened, and behold, a white horse. And He who sat on him was called Faithful and True, and in righteousness He judges and makes war. His eyes were like a flame of fire, and on His head were many crowns. He had a name written that no one knew except Himself. He was clothed with a robe dipped in blood, and His name is called the Word of God. (Revelation 19:11-13)

> ...when the Lord Yeshua is revealed from heaven with His mighty angels, in flaming fire taking vengeance on those who do not know God, and on those who do not obey the Good News of our Lord Yeshua the Messiah. (2 Thessalonians 1:7- 8)

> For I will gather all the nations to battle against Jerusalem; ...Then the LORD will go forth and fight against those nations, as He fights in the day of battle. And in that day His feet will stand on the Mount of Olives, which faces Jerusalem on the east... The people shall dwell in it [Jerusalem]; And no longer shall there be utter destruction, but Jerusalem shall be safely inhabited. And this shall be the plague with which the LORD will strike all the people who fought against Jerusalem: Their flesh shall dissolve while they stand on their feet, their eyes shall dissolve in their sockets, and their tongues shall dissolve in their mouths. (Zechariah 14:2-4, 11-12)

In that day, a nation shall be born in a day, and "thus all Israel will be saved" (Romans 11:26). Israel will be grafted back into her own olive tree and gathered and restored to the Lord (Romans 11:23-25).

Thus Yom Kippur, the Day of Atonement, serves to remind us that the gathering of Israel is coming. We are reminded also to share our faith in Messiah with Jewish people, and all people, with confidence that God is gathering Israel back to Himself. We may even now be planting seeds in the hearts of those Jewish people who will be among the 144,000. Let us not be merely religious, but truly restored to the Lord.

QUESTIONS FOR YOM KIPPUR:

1. In traditional Jewish communities, what are the ten
    days from Rosh Hashanah to Yom Kippur called? *High Holy Days*

2. Why did Daniel pray toward Jerusalem? *temple*

3. What does Solomon's prayer in 1 Kings 8:46-49 have
    to do with the need for blood atonement?

4. How could Yeshua fulfill the sacrifices since he does
    not fit the qualifications for any of the sacrifices
    given in the Torah (Hebrews 10)?

5. What the five steps of humble reconciliation to God?

6. Consider Zechariah 12 and Isaiah 53 in relationship
    to Yom Kippur.

5, 1 confession, 2 contrition, 3 repentance, 4 Jesus repays, 5 consecration to new life Compensation

GOD IS GATHERING
THE NATIONS

through

SUKKOT

CHAPTER 7

THE FEAST
OF BOOTHS

סוכות

THE SOURCE OF LIVING WATER

IN THE TORAH

Speak to the children of Israel, saying: "The fifteenth day of this seventh month shall be the Feast of Tabernacles for seven days to the LORD. On the first day there shall be a holy convocation. You shall do no customary work on it. For seven days you shall offer an offering made by fire to the LORD. On the eighth day you shall have a holy convocation, and you shall offer an offering made by fire to the LORD. It is a sacred assembly, and you shall do no customary work on it. These are the feasts of the LORD which you shall proclaim to be holy convocations, to offer an offering made by fire to the LORD, a burnt offering and a grain offering, a sacrifice and drink offerings, everything on its day – besides the Sabbaths of the LORD, besides your gifts, besides all your vows, and besides all your freewill offerings which you give to the LORD. Also on the fifteenth day of the seventh month, when you have gathered in the fruit of the land, you shall keep the feast of the LORD for seven days; on the first day there shall be a sabbath-rest, and on the eighth day a sabbath-rest. And you shall take for yourselves on the first day the fruit of beautiful trees, branches of palm trees, the boughs of leafy trees, and willows of the brook; and you shall rejoice before the LORD your God for seven days. You shall keep it as a feast to the LORD for seven days in the year. It shall be a statute forever in your generations. You shall celebrate it in the seventh month. You shall dwell in booths for seven days. All who are native Israelites shall dwell in booths, that your generations may know that I made the children of Israel dwell in booths when I brought them out of the land of Egypt: I am the LORD your God." So Moses declared to the children of Israel the feasts of the LORD. (Leviticus 23:34-44)

The final feast mentioned in Leviticus 23 is Sukkot[14], that is, the Feast of Booths (or as it is sometimes called, Tabernacles).

Sukkot is a harvest festival, also called the Feast of Ingathering[15]. In sharp contrast to the solemnity of Yom Kippur, five days earlier, this eight-day feast is occasionally referred to as *z'man simkhateinu,* "the season of our rejoicing." Seven days of continual, joyous celebration are followed by a solemn assembly on the eighth day, called *Shemini Atzeret* ("assembly of the eighth").

---

[14] pronounced "sue-*coat.*"
[15] Exodus 23:16, Leviticus 23:34- 43, Deuteronomy 16:13-15

The Sukkot festival is the culmination of all the feasts on God's redemptive calendar. Because of its place in the biblical calendar, by the time Solomon became king a few centuries after the giving of the Law, this festival had become the most important feast, and is simply called "the Feast" (1 Kings 8:2, 65). Israel is to live in booths each year, to remind us of the wilderness journey from Egypt to the Promised Land. As a harvest feast, it reminds us of our Sovereign God's wonderful provision for our lives. Both these ideas prophetically point to the end-time harvest ingathering of the Lord.

A contemporary Sukkot celebration consists of many ancient customs. These include waving the Four Species[16] toward the four corners of the earth, acknowledging the Lord as sovereign, reciting the *Hallel* Psalms[17], and most of all, living in booths. The word for "booth" is *sukkah*, which means covering or protection, although to the casual observer it would not appear to offer much protection at all. A *sukkah* is a frail, three-sided temporary dwelling. Homes throughout the community build their own booths, and often congregations will also put up a booth. For duration of the Feast of Booths, those who celebrate the holiday will pray, eat, and may even sleep in their *sukkah*.

SUKKOT IN THE OFF-SEASON

Though most believing congregations do not celebrate Sukkot, the New Covenant assumes some understanding of this important feast. In some cases, unless we understand the Jewish background of Scripture, we may actually

---

[16] Branches of palm, myrtle, willow, and a citron (Leviticus 23:40)

[17] Psalm 113 through 118

misunderstand the text in certain places. One key place is in Matthew's account of "the Transfiguration" of Messiah:

> Six days later Yeshua took with Him Peter and James and John his brother, and led them up on a high mountain by themselves. And He was transfigured before them; and His face shone like the sun, and His garments became as white as light. And behold, Moses and Elijah appeared to them, talking with Him. Then answered Peter, and said unto Yeshua, "Lord, it is good for us to be here; if You wish, I will make three booths here, one for You, and one for Moses, and one for Elijah." (Matthew 17:1-4)

We often chuckle at Peter for his impulsive, sometimes clumsy ways. He always wanted to say something. For instance, here Peter answered when no one had even asked a question. Be that as it may, in this case Peter knew what he was talking about. Note the previous context of this portion in Matthew 16:28:

> "Truly I say to you, there are some of those who are standing here who will not taste death until they see the Son of Man coming in His kingdom."

Some scholars doubt Yeshua for the statement that His disciples would see "the Son of Man coming in His kingdom," thinking He claimed that the end was coming in that very generation. Since the end did not come, they say that He is wrong. However, Sukkot helps us see what Yeshua and Matthew actually mean.

Yeshua says that some of His disciples would see His glorious kingdom appearance, not that all of them would. And the "some" refers to the three disciples Yeshua took with Him to the Mount. There, He reveals His Kingdom appearance and glory, and is transfigured before them. There, He speaks with Moses and Elijah— what a blessing for Moses, who had died just outside Israel, to finally make it into the Promised Land! Peter had a glimpse of the glorified King in the Messianic Kingdom.

And if Peter knew one thing for certain, it was that in the Kingdom, he would be celebrating the Feast of Booths! Therefore, he requested to make three booths for Yeshua, Moses and Elijah. Perhaps this was Peter's way of demonstrating his loyalty to Yeshua and honor for Him, and to make up for his lack of spiritual discernment when he had attempted to correct Him earlier (Matthew 16:22-23). In any case, Peter was acknowledging Messiah Yeshua as the Lord and true King of Israel, even if he did not fully comprehend Yeshua's need to suffer before being glorified (Matthew 16:21).

> While he was still speaking, a bright cloud overshadowed them, and behold, a voice out of the cloud said, "This is My beloved Son, with whom I am well pleased; listen to Him!" (Matthew 17:5)

The hope of the ages is the Kingdom of God, and Messiah was to bring in the Kingdom. As mentioned in the chapter on Passover, Yeshua's triumphal entry into Jerusalem, though it occurred in the spring time, is understood as another Sukkot event (John 12:12-16).

It was a common saying, "Until the dead revive and the Messiah, son of David, comes" (Sotah 48b). Since Yeshua had just raised Lazarus from the dead, the pilgrims were excited to think the Son of David had arrived, for the dead had actually been raised (John 11:44; 12:17-18).

another group expected a suffering servant

they wanted King David again

The people of Jerusalem were praising Yeshua as the King of Israel. They saw in Him the fulfillment of the hope of Israel– and of the world. Thus, the Pharisees saw this event demonstrating the "world" going after Yeshua (John 12:19). John further emphasized this aspect by mentioning the Greek-speaking Jews who, coming to Jerusalem for *Pesach*, and wanted to see Yeshua (John 12:20- 21). John recognized that this event anticipated the fulfillment of Sukkot, and at that time Messiah would be glorified as the world's Savior, Lord and King.

The prophet Zechariah provides vital information on how the first-century worshipper would look at Sukkot:

> Then it will come about that any who are left of all the nations that went against Jerusalem will go up from year to year to worship the King, the LORD of hosts, and to celebrate the Feast of Booths. And it will be that whichever of the families of the earth does not go up to Jerusalem to worship the King, the LORD of hosts, there will be no rain on them. If the family of Egypt does not go up or enter, then no rain will fall on them; it will be the plague with which the LORD smites the nations who do not go up to celebrate the Feast of Booths. This will be the punishment of Egypt, and the punishment of all the nations who do not go up to celebrate the Feast of Booths. (Zechariah 14:16-19)

When King Messiah reigns in His millennial kingdom upon His glorious throne in Jerusalem, we will all be celebrating the Feast of Booths. In fact, for those who would not celebrate Sukkot no water would be provided, for it would evidence their denial of the King's righteous reign and resistance to His universal authority. Sukkot celebration is serious business.

Therefore to the first century Jewish worshipper and in the Temple ceremonies, Sukkot became identified with the King reigning in His established Kingdom. This Feast anticipated the King's glorious reign not only over Israel, but over all nations. Israel would then be "the head and not the tail" (Deuteronomy 28:13), and the God of Israel would be glorified among His people. The prophet Ezekiel also envisioned for Israel this glorious future:

> I will make a covenant of peace with them; it will be an everlasting covenant with them. And I will place them and multiply them, and will set My sanctuary in their midst forever. My dwelling place also will be with them; and I will be their God, and they will be My people. And the nations will know that I am the LORD who sanctifies Israel, when My sanctuary is in their midst forever. (Ezekiel 37:26-28)

Think of the King reigning from Jerusalem in the restored Kingdom of Israel. No longer would the Romans or any other nation place Israel under their heel. Instead, they would all have to acknowledge the Lord as God, and Israel as His people. This harvest feast pictured a greater harvest of the nations and the Lord reigning as King over all. As the Feast of Ingathering, the prophetic aspect of Sukkot speaks of the ingathering of all nations to our God, acknowledging that He alone is sovereign and that in Him alone is their provision and security.

The seventy bulls sacrificed during the seven days of celebration were seen by early Jewish teachers as representing the nations of the world. As R. Eleazar stated:

70 nations

To what do those seventy bullocks [that were offered during the seven days of the Festival] correspond? To the seventy nations. To what does the single bullock [of the Eighth Day] correspond? To the unique nation. (Sukkah 55b)

That is why worshippers then and now wave the *lulav* to the four corners of the world. In the kingdom the Lord will be acknowledged by all as over all.

WATER AND SPIRIT

Now let's consider from John a Sukkot celebration which actually occurred at the normal time. John in particular saw Yeshua as inextricably linked to Sukkot, and to its fulfillment. They saw this in the way Yeshua utilized the ceremonies to reveal who He is, and to draw people to Himself.

In John 7:2 we see that the time of Sukkot was "at hand." Though Yeshua's brothers had taunted Him to go and reveal Himself early in the feast, Yeshua waited for the most opportune moment (John 7:1-10). It was at the height of the seventh day celebration, "on the last day, the great day of the feast" Yeshua was at the Temple in Jerusalem.

When the Temple stood there were biblical practices and unusual ceremonies that today are no longer conducted. In accordance with the Scriptures, Jerusalem was packed with the crowds of *lulav*-waving pilgrims that came from all over to celebrate the feast (Deuteronomy 16:16). There were special sacrifices in the Temple: thirteen bulls on the first day, twelve on the second day, eleven on the third day, ten on the fourth day, nine on the fifth day, eight on the sixth day, and seven on the seventh day (Numbers 29:13-32). This totalled seventy bulls in all, the number which was traditionally seen to represent all the nations.

However, we will consider two ancient Temple customs which have major significance for understanding the New Covenant. One such custom was the Temple water-pouring ceremony. Each day of the feast, a priest (*cohen*) came from the Temple down to the pool of Siloam carrying a golden pitcher. He was followed by those *lulav*-waving pilgrims who had come to Jerusalem to celebrate Sukkot.

The priest would fill the golden pitcher with water from the pool and return to the Temple followed by crowds chanting from Isaiah, "we will gather water from the wells of salvation" (Isaiah 12:3), and from the Psalms, "*Hoshiaynu*" transliterated "Hosanna," meaning "save us now" (Psalm 118:22-24). The priest would make one circuit around the altar and then pour out the water praying for God to provide what He alone could give.

The priest would do this each day for the first six days of the festival, but the seventh day of the feast would be different. The seventh day was considered the great day of the feast, because the eighth day was a solemn assembly, without any of the joyous celebration of the previous seven. Therefore the seventh day was called, "The Great Hosanna" (*Hoshanna Rabba*). On the seventh day the priest would go to the pool of Siloam with his golden pitcher, followed by the praising and worshipping crowds. He would return to the Temple as before, but now the priest would circle the altar seven times. With each circuit the crowds would grow louder and louder in their cry for the provision and salvation of God.[18]

Do you wonder what this water-pouring ceremony has to do with a harvest festival? One might imagine a naturalistic rationale, such as the need for water for the next growing season, but the issue is actually much more profound. After all, for the first-century worshipper in Jerusalem, Sukkot had special meaning. Consider what the prophet declared, from the Sukkot passage we read:

> And the LORD will be King over all the earth; in that day the LORD will be the only one, and His name the only one. (Zechariah 14:9)

In the kingdom, under the Lord's reign, it is not only water that will be provided. For as much as water is desperately needed in the arid Middle East, there is a much greater need for the human soul. The prophets seize on this connection clearly:

> For I will pour out water on the thirsty land and streams on the dry ground; I will pour out My Spirit on your offspring and My blessing on your descendants. (Isaiah 44:3)

> I will not hide My face from them any longer, for I will have poured out My Spirit on the house of Israel, declares the Lord GOD. (Ezekiel 39:29)

> I will pour out on the house of David and on the inhabitants of Jerusalem, the Spirit of grace and of supplication, so that they will look on Me whom they have pierced. (Zechariah 12:10)

---

[18] In Talmud, see Sukkah 34a, 54b, 48b, 51a; Rosh Hashanah 16a

Therefore each year at Sukkot, the Temple water-pouring ceremony symbolized and anticipated the Spirit of God being "poured out" even as the prophets predicted. The ceremony pictured one of the most anticipated aspects of the Kingdom: the provision of God's unifying Spirit for His people.

A TORRENTIAL OUTPOURING

Let us picture this crucial point. Again, it was the final day of the feast. The priest had just finished his seventh circuit around the Temple altar. He is pouring out the water with his golden pitcher, praying for God's provision, and as thousands of people are crying out "Hosanna! Save us now!" for the salvation of God— suddenly, Yeshua proclaims, loudly above the din of the people:

> If anyone is thirsty, let him come to Me and drink. He who believes in Me, as the Scripture said, "From his innermost being will flow rivers of living water." But this He spoke of the Spirit, whom those who believed in Him were to receive; for the Spirit was not yet given, because Yeshua was not yet glorified. (John 7:37-39)

Yeshua declared Himself to be the fulfillment of the promise of the God for Israel and the world, the true hope for Sukkot. Are you spiritually dry? Cry out to Yeshua the Messiah, and be satisfied by His grace and love. Maybe you came to Him many years ago, but today you are dried out. In the text the word "come" is in the present tense, thus we are to come to Him, and to keep coming to Him. The circumstances we go through are often more than enough to dry us out spiritually, and leave us feeling like a desert.

We are to come to Him, trusting and relying upon Him for the grace that He alone can provide, which is sufficient for all our wilderness experiences.

Messiah promises those who come to Him that, "out of his innermost being will flow rivers [literally, "torrents"] of living waters" (John 7:38). When He said this He was referring to Isaiah:

> The Lord will continually guide you, and satisfy your desire in scorched places, and give strength to your bones; and you will be like a watered garden, and like a spring of water whose waters will not fail. (Isaiah 58:11)

Have you ever noticed that after a severe drought when it rains heavily there are no puddles of water left on the ground? Why? There was not enough rain to saturate the ground, much less produce any excess or overflow. That is the point Yeshua is making.

No matter how long your spiritual drought has been going on, the Scripture promises that there will not only be enough of Messiah's all sufficient grace for your life, but that there will be an overflow. Indeed, torrents of living water will flow to you and through you into the lives of those around you. In fact, perhaps you are in those tough situations now just so the Lord can use you to water a few dry lawns in your community, family, school, or work place.

We all go through our share of afflictions, but believers in Yeshua are to "come to Him" and find sufficient grace for our lives. As we share Him we overflow into the lives of others around us. Remember, Sukkot pictured that the

King not only had to be reigning, but honored (Zechariah 14:17). You may believe in Yeshua, but does the King reign in your heart? Are we looking to Him for what He alone can provide?

In John 7:39 we understand where this provision is found, "But this He spoke of the Spirit, whom those who believed in Him were to receive; for the Spirit was not yet given, because Jesus was not yet glorified." Chronologically, this speaks of Yeshua's ascension to the right hand of the Father, and the subsequent outpouring of the Holy Spirit on the day of Pentecost (Acts 2). But in our personal lives, we see that when Yeshua is glorified then the Spirit is given.

When does the Holy Spirit provide the spiritual resource of love, joy, and peace that we need for our daily lives? The Holy Spirit (*Ruach HaKodesh*) does not produce fruit without our working on the root, which is faith and dependence upon the Lord and His Word. When we acknowledge Him in all our ways He will make our paths straight (Proverbs 3:6). In your situations and sufferings, look to Yeshua as you run the race that is set before you; trusting in Him, and He will bring it to pass. Sukkot reminds us that when the King reigns on the throne, God's provision is there for His people.

When Yeshua is glorified, the Spirit is given, and rivers of living water will flow into the lives of others. This is the very truth that the New Covenant declares has happened in Messiah. For even as Messiah was poured out unto death for our sins, so He has poured out the Holy Spirit to all who believe on Him.

LIGHT AND SALVATION

We've looked at the symbol of water in Sukkot, especially in the Spirit's soul-satisfying ministry in the lives of believers in Yeshua. Light is another Biblical symbol, and another unusual Sukkot ceremony that took place in the first century Jerusalem Temple. It centered around gigantic golden candlesticks.

On the first day of Sukkot, three seventy-five foot high candlesticks were erected in The Court of the Women where the treasury was located. This is the very same treasury where Messiah noted a poor widow who gave her sacrificial gift (Mark 12:41-42). The Court of the Women was a place where all could come to give their gifts.

Here all worshippers, men and women alike could enter and experience the joy of Sukkot around the great candlesticks. The light from those huge candles was reported to give light to all the courtyards of Jerusalem. The wicks for these candles were made from the priests' old garments, and in order to light them, young men would climb seventy-five feet up several ladders. At the base of the candles we read from the Talmud:

> Men of piety and good deeds would dance before them with lighted torches in their hands, singing songs and praises. Levites without number played harps, lyres, cymbals trumpets and other musical instruments there upon the fifteen steps leading down from the Court of the Gentiles to the Court of the Women. (Sukkah 51 a-b; 53a)

These celebrations would continue for the full seven days. On the eighth day the lights were extinguished for a holy and solemn assembly.

Light was a reminder of God's revelation and His guidance:

> Who will show us any good? Lift up the light of Your countenance upon us, O LORD. (Psalm 4:6)

> For You light my lamp; the LORD my God illumines my darkness. (Psalm 18:28)

> The LORD is my light and my salvation. (Psalm 27:1)

> The LORD is God, and He has given us light. (Psalm 118:27)

> The poor man and the oppressor have this in common: the LORD gives light to the eyes of both. (Proverbs 29:13)

> Though I dwell in darkness, the LORD is a light for me. (Micah 7:8)

As the Lord was Israel's light and guide in the wilderness so He will be their light when the Lord as King reigns in the kingdom. As the prophet Isaiah describes:

> Come, house of Jacob, and let us walk in the light of the LORD. (Isaiah 2:5)

> Arise, shine; for your light has come, and the glory of the LORD has risen upon you. (Isaiah 60:1)

The light of the giant candlesticks pictured the future kingdom that Isaiah and Zechariah predicted:

> No longer will you have the sun for light by day, nor for brightness will the moon give you light; but you will have the LORD for an everlasting light, and your God for your glory. Your sun will no longer set, nor will your moon wane; for you will have the LORD for an

everlasting light, and the days of your mourning will be over. (Isaiah 60:19,20)

In that day there will be no light; the luminaries will dwindle. For it will be a unique day which is known to the LORD, neither day nor night, but it will come about that at evening time there will be light. (Zechariah 14:6-7)

The New Covenant makes mention of the prophecy in Isaiah 60:19-20 as it focuses our attention to the eternal period when the Lord is our everlasting light.

But I saw no temple in it, for the Lord God Almighty and the Lamb are its temple. The city had no need of the sun or of the moon to shine in it, for the glory of God illuminated it. The Lamb is its light. (Revelation 21:22-23; see also 22:5)

Traditionally, the present age is referred to as *Olam HaZeh*, and the future age is simply referred to as *Olam HaBa*, which means the world to come or the days of Messiah. In *Olam HaZeh* we may need various lights, but those Temple candles pictured the hope of an age in which no other light but the Lord will be needed. The Kingdom to which Sukkot pointed was to be a time when we would no longer walk in the darkness of sin. Rather we would walk in the gladness, salvation and freedom of the Lord's light. It was prophesied in Isaiah that the Messiah of Israel was to be the light to all the nations of the world:

I am the LORD, I have called you in righteousness, I will also hold you by the hand and watch over you, and I will appoint you as a covenant to the people, as a light to the nations... It is too small a thing that You should be My

Servant to raise up the tribes of Jacob and to restore the preserved ones of Israel; I will also make You a light of the nations so that My salvation may reach to the end of the earth. (Isaiah 42:6, 49:6)

Though the majority of rabbis did not accept Yeshua as the promised Messiah, this was their understanding as well, "Though I sit in darkness, ... yet, the Lord is light unto me, in the days of Messiah" (Sukkah 2a). It is confirmed in many other places this understanding of Messiah as the Light of Israel:

Let the righteous rejoice in the building of Thy city and the establishment of the temple and in the exalting of the horn of David Thy servant and the preparation of a light for the son of Jesse Thy Messiah. (Berachoth 29a)

"In thy light we see light." What is this light which the congregation of Israel looks for? That is the light of Messiah, as it is said, "God saw the light and it was good." (Peskita Rabbati, 161a-161b, 162a-162b, AD 650-900)

God replied: "No, only until the sun appears" (ib.), that is, till the coming of the Messiah; for it says, "But unto you that fear My name shall the sun of righteousness arise with healing in its wings" (Malachi 3:20 Heb.). (Exodus Rabbah 31:10)

APPRECIATE THE LIGHT

We have seen that Sukkot pictures the fulfillment of God's redemption for Israel and the world. Therefore, it was at Sukkot that Yeshua went up to the Temple and declared Himself to be not only the life-giving fulfillment of the Feast, but the light-giving fulfillment as well.

Remember, the pilgrims who attended Sukkot from around the world had been celebrating joyously for seven days. On the eighth day was the solemn assembly. With the lights from the great Sukkot candles extinguished, how dim it must have appeared after such a brilliant and joyous celebration! Perhaps the pilgrims had hoped that it would be different this year, that the longed for tradition would be fulfilled. Yet the great lights were put out, a reminder of their dimmed hopes as well.

It was then and there that Messiah spoke. John is careful to note the location, "These words He spoke in the treasury, as He taught in the temple" (John 8:20). There at the treasury in the Court of the Women, near the great but extinguished candles, Yeshua declared:

> "I am the Light of the world; he who follows Me will not walk in the darkness, but will have the Light of life." (John 8:12)

Messiah is the Light:

- *He is the Personal Light of God*: By saying, "I am..." He indicated that He alone is the revelation of God's glory.

- *He is the Perpetual Light of God*, as Yeshua professed to be the only inexhaustible source of spiritual nourishment, or the "Light of life." The candlesticks were to be extinguished after the feast, but His light would remain.

- *He is the Perfect Light of God*, "the Light" by which eternal direction could be established for our lives, so that we might not "walk in the darkness."

- *He is the Pure Light of God*, the clarification of God and truth, the genuine light by which truth and falsehood can be distinguished (John 1:9).

- *He is the Powerful Light of God*, "the Light of the world," able to make the difference for everyone. Regardless of culture and heritage, all people need His light.

APPROPRIATE THE LIGHT

Messiah also tells us we need to possess the Light, for in Him we shall have the light of life. Many times we think that if we ever really need the Lord, such as when catastrophe, illness, or death comes, we can then get what we need. However, it is better to have the resource five years too soon, than five minutes too late. Marriages need spiritual insight; child rearing needs moral discernment; businesses need enlightened standards; and in this world of temptations we all need spiritual guidance.

APPLY THE LIGHT

Finally, Messiah tells us we need to pursue the light. "He who follows Me." That is, we are to apply the light in our lives. What does it actually mean to follow Yeshua? Biblically, the word "follow" is used several ways:

- As a *soldier*, to follow Him in purity, following Him alone– just as "the armies which are in heaven, clothed in fine linen, were following Him on white horses" (Revelation 19:14). The concern of following is not where I am going, but who I am following. I am to follow Him wherever– "These are the ones who follow the Lamb wherever He goes" (Revelation 14:4). Therefore whatever He commands, we do.

- As a *servant*, follow Him in service– "If anyone serves Me, he must follow Me" (John 12:26). We follow the Lord, whenever He calls, wherever He leads. If Yeshua is our Light, we follow as His servants.

- As our *standard*, we follow Him through suffering– "Messiah also suffered for you, leaving you an example for you to follow in His steps" (1 Peter 2:21).

- As a *student*, follow Him in the truth– "the sound doctrine which you have been following (1 Timothy 4:6). Not why, but who! The student follows the teacher's line of reasoning. When I follow Him, His word is a lamp unto my feet. During World War II when the Italian army captured Libya, they tortured some of their Lybian prisoners. When the Libyans had captured Italian soldiers they wanted to torture the Italians. The Libyan leader stopped them. "But why?" they complained. "They torture us!" The leader responded, "But they are not our teachers." In a similar way, believers are not to follow the world's example, but to follow the Lord.

If you are not following Messiah Yeshua, who, or what are you following?

- *Stubbornness*– "a rebellious people, following their own thoughts" (Isaiah 65:2).

- *Trivial pursuits*– "he who follows frivolous pursuits will have poverty in plenty" (Proverbs 28:19).

- *Vanity*– "foolish prophets are following their own spirit and have seen nothing" (Ezekiel 13:3).

- *Hedonism*– "Many will follow their sensuality" (2 Peter 2:2); "mockers will come following after their own lusts" (2 Peter 3:3).

LIVING IN THE LIGHT

One can actually have light, and not use it. The fifteenth century Cathedral of Florence Italy has a small aperture at the top of its dome. Each year on the twenty first of June the sunlight comes through the aperture and hits squarely on a brass plate on the floor. If the light does not cover the brass plate fully, there is concern that the building has shifted, and foundation work must begin at once. Yeshua said, "He who follows Me will not walk in the darkness." If I do not follow His teaching in all areas, I will not enjoy His provision for my life.

It is said of the blind musician, Ray Charles that he lives in his home without ever turning on the lights. Only when sighted friends come over does he use the lights. You see, one can tell the blind from the sighted not by those who have lights, but by those who actually use them. Many homes have Bibles, but who actually reads them? Many have heard of Messiah, but who actually follows Him?

Yeshua is the only Light worth following. So if you have the light, turn it on! Appreciate the Light— He alone is the light of the world. Appropriate the Light— have the light in your soul by trusting in Yeshua! And finally, apply the light— by following Yeshua daily you will never walk in darkness, but have the "Light of Life."

MESSIAH, THE ETERNAL SUKKAH

Now that we have considered the themes of water and light, let us turn our attention to the most basic part of Sukkot: the *sukkah* itself! Let's return to the Torah. Leviticus shows us how when we came out of Egypt we were weak, vulnerable, and dependent upon God, just like the frail appearance of the *sukkah*.

> You shall dwell in booths for seven days. All who are native Israelites shall dwell in booths, that your generations may know that I made the children of Israel dwell in booths when I brought them out of the land of Egypt: I am the LORD your God. (Leviticus 23:42-43)

In the wilderness we appeared easily conquerable by the desert tribes living there (Exodus 17:9-16), but the Lord was the secret resource for Israel's wilderness victory.

As Israel was redeemed from Egyptian bondage by God's power, so they are kept through the wilderness trials by God's power. Just as there were no works of your own to redeem you, there are no works that can keep you. It is all the sovereign work of God. At Sukkot we are reminded of Passover, where we see the secret to enjoying both the sufficiency and security the Lord has for our lives. The booth pictures not only Israel's freedom from bondage, but her true security in God.

Today, along our 'wilderness journey,' reliance upon Him is still our hope and protection. Sukkot teaches that the people of God can never live as if we could manage spiritually on our own (Leviticus 23:43). We need the Lord. He is our sufficiency, and in Him we have the protection of God. As illustrated in the wilderness, our protection is in the Lord, for He Himself is our booth. As John writes:

> In the beginning was the Word, and the Word was with God, and the Word was God... And the Word was

made flesh, and dwelt among us [tabernacled], and we beheld his glory, the glory as of the only begotten of the Father, full of grace and truth. (John 1:1, 14)

The Greek word used for "dwelt" among us is *skeine,* which is the verb form for the *sukkah,* alluding to Sukkot. Messiah appeared weak, frail, flimsy, just as a booth would appear. Little did people realize that beneath that ordinary exterior was the fullness of the omnipotent *El Shaddai,* God Almighty, the Holy One of Israel.

OUR PROTECTION IN THE SUKKAH

The word *sukkah* means to cover, as in protection. Here are some examples of where this word is used. When Moses asked the Lord to show him His glory, God said to Moses:

Behold, there is a place by me, and you shall stand upon a rock: And it shall come to pass, while my glory passes by, that I will put you in a cleft of the rock, and will *cover* you with my hand while I pass by." (Exodus 33:21-22)

God's hand was Moses' *sukkah* in the cleft of the rock. David praised God with this song of deliverance from Psalm 140:7, "O GOD the Lord, the strength of my salvation, thou hast *covered* my head in the day of battle." Whatever victory David achieved, the Lord was a *sukkah* of protection in the battle.

In the Kingdom, Messiah, as "the Branch of the Lord," will reign from Jerusalem, as pictured prophetically in the feast of Sukkot. This protection will again be Israel's to enjoy as a nation:

In that day shall the branch of the LORD be beautiful and glorious... And the LORD will create upon every dwelling place of mount Zion, and upon her assemblies, a cloud and smoke by day, and the shining of a flaming fire by night: for upon all the glory shall be a defense. And there shall be a tabernacle for a shadow in the daytime from the heat, and for a place of refuge, and for a covert from storm and from rain. (Isaiah 4:2-6)

When the Scripture promises, "there shall be a tabernacle" that, too, is the *sukkah*. In the Kingdom, Messiah will be all the protection Israel or any nation will ever need. Our security is found not in the largest synagogue or church, not in our own abilities or possessions, but in Him, our *Sukkah*.

Though to the world we may look weak and frail, in Messiah we are secure and strong. He will cover and protect us. Paul seems to hint at this very idea when he writes, "Therefore if anyone is in Messiah, he is a new creature; the old things passed away; behold, new things have come" (2 Corinthians 5:17).

In Him we are new creations, but only in Yeshua. Whether in war or wilderness, in Yeshua our *Sukkah*, and in Him alone, we are secure. God has fully provided our salvation and new life.

JUST PASSING THROUGH

There is an additional reason God wants future generations to remember the wilderness experience. Sukkot testifies to the transitional nature of this world, and helps us remember the temporary nature of this life. There was no true rest in the wilderness. The booth itself had to be a temporary dwelling, we are to "dwell in a temporary abode" (Leviticus 23:42).

When you live in booths you testify to your neighbors that this world is temporary and is not your home; we are all just passing through. Whatever you and I own now will one day pass away. My certain hope is to one day be with God, in the true Promised Land of Heaven. Even the Patriarch Abraham had this hope.

> By faith he [Abraham] lived as an alien in the land of promise, as in a foreign land, dwelling in tabernacles with Isaac and Jacob, fellow heirs of the same promise. For he looked forward to the city that has foundations, whose architect and builder is God. (Hebrews 11:9-10)

All of *Olam HaZeh* is like the wilderness. Therefore, just as we were not to live as permanent residents of the wilderness, so let us not live as though this temporal world is our permanent home. Like Abraham, we also look forward to our Heavenly home, which our Lord has gone ahead of us to prepare:

> Yeshua said, "In my Father's house are many mansions: if it were not so, I would have told you. I go to prepare a place for you. And if I go and prepare a place for you, I will come again, and receive you unto myself; that where I am, there ye may be also." (John 14:2-3)

One day we will be in the very presence of the Lord, and still Sukkot will be pictured as the eternal hope of all who believe in Yeshua. Revelation 7 states, those "from every nation" will be standing before the throne of God and waving "palm branches in their hands." (Revelation 7:9) There will be no more hunger, thirst, or weeping because "the Lamb in the center of the throne will be their shepherd, and will guide them to springs of the water of life; and God will wipe every tear from their eyes" (Revelation 7:17). Why will this be so fulfilling? We will be covered by "the Lord's tabernacle [*sukkah*]" (Revelation 7:15).

Every nation, tribe, people, and language will give honor and praise to Yeshua, the Lamb, the Lord of hosts, "when He comes, in that day, to be glorified in His saints and to be admired among all those who believe" (2 Thessalonians 1:10). This will happen because Messiah our Sukkah will dwell among us:

> And I heard a loud voice from the throne, saying, "Behold, the tabernacle of God is among men, and He will dwell among them, and they shall be His people, and God Himself will be among them, and be their God." (Revelation 21:3)

Sukkot pictures and promises what a glorious time this will be, when the biblical hope of "peace on earth" will finally be realized internationally and forever.

✡   ✡   ✡

Carly Simon — Bring New Jerusalem

Through these Fall Appointments we see what the future holds for Israel and all believers in Messiah. Thus we can anticipate the prophetic events pictured in these three great gatherings of God:

The Feast of Trumpets– the gathering of the Body of Messiah to the Lord.

Yom Kippur– the gathering of Israel to be restored the Lord.

Sukkot– the gathering of all nations to glorify Yeshua, the King of Kings and Lord of Lords.

The Feast of Trumpets reminds us to be ready for His imminent return. Are you ready for His return? Yom Kippur reminds us of the need to be restored to Him through His atonement. Finally the Feast of Booths reminds us that the Lord is to be reigning over every life that trusts in Him. If we have responded by faith in Yeshua, we are ready for Him, we are restored to Him, and we are ruled by Him, even as we will reign with Him for eternity.

STUDY QUESTIONS:

1. What are the Four Species?

2. What did the *sukkah* in the wilderness symbolize?

3. Why was it thought that Sukkot pointed to the future Messianic Kingdom?

4. Describe two instances of Sukkot being anticipated "out of season" in the New Covenant Scriptures.

5. Describe the water pouring ceremony. What were the pilgrims crying out during the water pouring ceremony of Sukkot?

6. How does Messiah's declaration "I am the Light of the World" relate to the festival of Sukkot at the Temple in Jerusalem?

7. How is Yeshua our *sukkah*?

GOD IS GIVING VICTORY TO HIS PEOPLE

through

HANUKKAH

CHAPTER 8

THE FEAST OF DEDICATION

חנוכה

THE LIGHT OF THE WORLD

The Feast of Dedication was established as a memorial to the purification and rededication of the temple in Jerusalem in the Jewish month of Kislev 25, 165 BCE which took exactly three years to the date from its defilement. Antiochus Epiphanes, the king of Syria, had captured Jerusalem, plundered the temple treasury, and to add insult to injury, profaned the temple by sacrificing a pig to Zeus on the temple altar (Daniel 8:9-14). His attempt to Hellenize[1] Judea resulted in what is known as the revolt of the Maccabees. Led by Mattathias Maccabee and his

---

1 To "Hellenize" the Jewish people, Antiochus Epiphanes forced them to conform to Greek culture and religion. Under penalty of death, Jews were prohibited from Biblical worship, circumcision, and Torah study (171-165BCE).

five sons, the Israelites resisted and fought against the occupying Syrian army, and after three years, the Israelites defeated the Syrians and liberated the Jewish people.

THE LEGEND OF THE OIL

Hanukkah is the Hebrew word for dedication. Hanukkah is thought by many people to be eight days long because of a legend regarding the oil in the Temple.

According to this tradition, when the Maccabees recaptured and rededicated the Temple, they attempted to light the Temple menorah. This menorah, which was to burn continually, represented the eternal light of God. Alas, the Talmud relates, there was only enough oil to last for one day. The oil miraculously lasted eight days when the Temple was rededicated.

This legend probably developed during the Roman occupation long after the events occurred. Why? Some think that the legend of the oil became popular in order to avoid the warlike aspects of the holiday. After all, celebrating the overthrow of your oppressors might be perceived as "politically incorrect" by the Roman army! It would likely have caused unwanted trouble for the Israelites of that day.

The historical reason for eight days is actually based on Sukkot, the Feast of Booths.

> The Jews celebrated joyfully for eight days as on the Feast of Booths, remembering how a little while before, they had spent the feast of Booths living like wild animals in caves on the mountains. Carrying rods entwined with leaves, green branches and palms, they sang hymns of grateful praise to Him who had brought about the purification of His own Place. (2 Maccabees 10:6-7)

The Feast of Sukkot was the most recent Feast in the calendar when the Temple was rededicated for holy worship, but during the last three celebrations they were engaged in guerrilla warfare. However, they recognized the Lord's provision and protection in bringing them victory. Like Hezekiah's later, greater Passover, Hanukkah was originally considered like a second Sukkot for the victorious Jewish army (2 Chronicles 30). Even the theme of light, so central to Hanukkah, came from Sukkot.[2]

Today, despite what some may think, the Feast of Dedication is more than a gift-giving alternative to Christmas. Hanukkah is a joyous holiday to be sure, but it is meant to celebrate the victory God gave our people through the heroic efforts of the Maccabeean family.

Among the festivities and symbols associated with Hanukkah, one of the best-known is the children's game called *dreidel*. A *dreidel* is a four-sided top with a Hebrew letter on each side that form an acrostic for the phrase "A Great Miracle Happened There." In Israel, the *dreidel* is a little different. The acrostic says "A Great Miracle Happened Here." To play the game, the children spin the top remembering the historical event when once again, our people were saved from destruction.

During the eight days of Hanukkah there is a menorah that is lit as well. The Hanukkah menorah, called a *hanukiyah*, has nine candleholders, rather than seven. Eight of the candles are lit for each night of Hanukkah, and the ninth is called the *shamash*, which is Hebrew for servant. The *shamash* or servant candle is lit first and is then used to light the other candles, increasing by one

---

[2] see chapter 7

each night successively. Foods traditionally enjoyed on Hanukkah include: *latkes* (potato pancakes fried in oil, my favorite) and in Israel, jelly donuts (my wife Miriam's favorite). Though considered by many as merely a minor Jewish holiday, Hanukkah contains profound biblical truths for all people to seriously consider.

MESSIAH'S HANUKKAH MESSAGE

You may find it surprising that the only place in the Bible where the festival of Hanukkah is specifically mentioned is in the New Covenant:

> At that time the Feast of the Dedication took place at Jerusalem; it was winter, and Yeshua was walking in the Temple in the portico of Solomon. (John 10:22-23)

At that time Yeshua was teaching in Jerusalem at the Temple at Solomon's colonnade, or Solomon's porch. According to the historian Josephus, the eastern part of the walkway surrounded the outer court of Herod's Temple. The portico served as a shelter from the heat of the sun in summer and from the cold rain in winter. Yeshua used this as a center for informal teaching and preaching since there were always people present for worship at the temple.

It was here in the context of Hanukkah, that Yeshua taught that faith in Him is the victory. It was no coincidence that Yeshua delivered this revealing truth about Himself at this time. John understood that Yeshua is the true Deliverer of our people. The teaching that Messiah presents demonstrates that Yeshua identified His own redemptive work with Hanukkah.

The Maccabees cleansed the Temple that it might be used for holy worship and God's glory, whereas Yeshua cleanses us from our sins that we might be a sacred temple for holy worship to the glory of God (1 Corinthians 6:18-20). The yearly celebration of this historic victory gives the backdrop of Yeshua's Hanukkah message.

> The Judeans then gathered around Him and were saying to Him, "How long will You keep us in suspense? If you are the Messiah, tell us plainly." (John 10:24)

Certain occasions raise certain issues. After the victory of Hanukkah, defiled stones from the altar which had been desecrated by Antiochus were kept "in a convenient place on the Temple hill until there should come a prophet to tell what to do with them" (1 Maccabees 4:44-47). In these so-called silent years, the people awaited a prophet. Also, every Hanukkah the Jewish people were looking for the Messiah, the Greater Maccabee, to come and give them deliverance from yet another enemy. So for Judeans in Jerusalem under the Roman heel, this question of "Messiah" would mean: "Where is the Redeemer to deliver us from our Roman oppressors?"

"Yeshua answered them, 'I told you, and you believed not: the works that I do in My Father's name, they bear witness of Me'" (John 10:25). Why didn't Yeshua just give a "plain" answer? Because He knew the issues of the day.

The Scriptures prophesied that Messiah's first coming would be for the purpose of making the atoning sacrifice for our sins. They described Messiah as the suffering servant, as well as the King who will rule (Isaiah 53; Psalm 2). The rabbis interpreted this to mean that there would be not one, but two Messiahs. The suffering Messiah, who was believed to die in battle, they called *Moshiach ben Yoseph* (Messiah, Son of Joseph), and the reigning Messiah to rule over Israel and the Nations, they called *Moshiach ben David* (Messiah, Son of David). It was the "Son of David" type which people were expecting.

If Yeshua had merely answered "yes," He would have been accommodating Himself to the political idea that they were expecting, though it is at His second coming that Messiah brings judgment upon the enemies of God and the enemies of His people. On the other hand, if He said "no," He would have been denying the truth!

Messiah wisely responds, "I've already told you"—in words and deeds (John 10:25). He tells them to check His words and His works. His words proved that He is a "prophet like unto Moses." Therefore they must listen to Him (Deuteronomy 18:15). His works were miraculous, even more so than Hanukkah's miracles.

> If I do not the works of My Father, believe Me not. But if I do, though ye believe not Me, believe the works: that ye may know, and believe, that the Father is in Me, and I in Him. (John 10:37-38)

Yeshua wanted the people of His day to see His miracles— healing, deliverance, and even resurrection of the dead— and believe in Him as a result. His miracles point to His Messianic identity. Yeshua Himself personifies the message of Hanukkah, that God is actively involved in the affairs of His people.

We must have faith in what is revealed, not merely in what we think we need. God provides the eternal salvation that we truly need, not merely the temporary solutions that we desire.

An old acquaintance of mine was healed of a terrible disease, and therefore believed and testified throughout the New York area about Yeshua, his Healer. But when the illness returned, he became bitter and denied the Lord. Do we place our faith in God's Word, or in our own experiences? The Maccabees pointed to the desecrated temple and the oppressive Syrians and said, "Let us defeat them and rededicate the temple." Short term faith was required. However, Yeshua says that we are the desecrated temple, and that we need to be cleansed and rededicated so that we might walk with God.

Messiah required greater faith from His followers. Sometimes it is easier to blame the circumstances, such as the oppressive Romans or the Syrians, but it takes faith in God to realize that He can deliver us through our difficulties.

THE TRUE SHEPHERD OF ISRAEL

My sheep hear My voice, and I know them, and they follow Me: And I give unto them eternal life; and they shall never perish, neither shall any man pluck them out of My hand. (John 10:27-28)

The Messiah is not only the Redeemer of Israel; He is their True Shepherd. Those who hear His voice are His sheep and they have faith in Him: "My sheep hear My voice." His sheep are also His followers, "They follow Me." There is a mutual recognition and reciprocal action. The picture of faith is in following– as in following a teacher's line of reasoning, or perspective. We follow the way He looks at the issues of life. We understand our lives from His perspective and therefore, act accordingly.

Messiah's sheep live forever: "I give unto them eternal life" (John 10:28). There is guaranteed assurance of life eternal.

How is it a guarantee? First, His Word is trustworthy, contrary to man's insincerity. Many others have claimed falsely to give and to gain eternal life. Yeshua promises what He alone can give and deliver.

Secondly, His Word is truth, contrary to people's ideas. It's true that we may not comprehend this matter of eternal life. Some think that their eternal rest is in a coffin! However, the truth is not relative, nor is it dependent on our comprehension.

Eternal life is a totally new kind of existence for believers. Yes, the life Yeshua gives us is never-ending, but this is because God's own life is without end. This life is of superlative quality, because God's own life is of superlative quality. Messiah imparts to us both the quality and quantity of God's own life, because through Him all the fullness of God dwells within us. Eternal life is His life in us.

I was born in the flesh in 1948; I was born of the Spirit in 1972. Someday you will hear Sam Nadler is dead. Do not believe a word of it. At that moment I shall be more alive than I am now. I shall have gone higher, out of this feeble shack into a house that is immortal, a body that neither sin nor sickness can corrupt or kill, a body fashioned like unto His glorious body.

That which is born of the flesh may die; that which is born of the Spirit will live forever, and in Yeshua, I live! The Maccabees brought deliverance, but only for a short while, for they could not deliver us from either the Romans or even the Maccabbee's own corruption once they got into power! In contrast, Messiah brings deliverance forever, and gives eternal life. How does this happen?

My Father, which gave them to Me, is greater than all; and no man is able to pluck them out of My Father's hand. I and the Father are one. (John 10:29, 30)

The point in this portion is this: since "My Father...is greater than all," as all would acknowledge; and since "I and the Father are one," as His sheep would acknowledge; therefore if you are one of His sheep, you are secure in Yeshua's hand. A deeper look into the Hebrew further reveals Messiah's deity. When it says, "I and the Father are One" (*Ani v'ha'Av, echad anachnu*) the word for "One" is the same word that is used in the *Shema*: "Hear O Israel the Lord our God, the Lord is One" (*Shema Yisrael Adonai Eloheinu Adonai Echad*) (Deuteronomy 6:4). Yeshua's self-assertion of His own divinity is occasioned by His regard for His followers: "No one will snatch them from My [Yeshua's] hand" or the "Father's hand" (John 10:29). Therefore, we who are in Yeshua's care have complete assurance that nothing "will be able to separate us from the love of God which comes to us through Messiah Yeshua our Lord" (Romans 8:38-39).

Did Yeshua really mean that He is God come in the flesh? Yes! The Judeans once again picked up stones in order to stone him, as they had done in John 8:59, and for the same reason: they misunderstood His self-identification as God to be blasphemy (John 10:33, Philippians 2:6-10). C.S. Lewis has made this point well:

"A man who was merely a man and said the sort of things Jesus said would not be a great moral teacher. He would either be a lunatic — on the level with the man who says he is a poached egg — or else he would be the Devil of Hell. You must make your choice. Either this man was, and is, the Son of God, or else a madman or something worse. ... let us not come with any patronising nonsense about his being a great human teacher. He has not left that open to us. He did not intend to... "

FOLLOWING IS THE VICTORY

The application of Yeshua's message for our lives is this: Victory is faith in the Father's greatness. Are you facing a Goliath size problem? There is One who is greater than Goliath. Remember that defeat is measuring your life by the size of your problem, but victory comes when you measure life's challenges by the size of your God. If Yeshua is less than the eternal Savior, then we have something less than eternal salvation. Despite the temporary trials and tribulations, there is an ultimate victory in Messiah, our Savior for Eternity.

As great as the Maccabees victory was, it was only temporary. By contrast, Messiah is the greater Maccabee. He is not a temporary fix, but brings permanent victory. Yes, He demands greater loyalty than the Maccabees, since He provides greater security than the Maccabees. Trust Him as the Savior, Shepherd, and the Son of God. Yeshua is the Victor, and following Him brings the victory.

We can see that Messiah not only celebrated but capitalized on Hanukkah to speak of what He alone can do. He came to dedicate the true Temple of God, that is, each of us who would believe in Him (1 Corinthians 6:19-20). Through Messiah, Hanukkah teaches us what it means to be truly dedicated to the Lord.

The word "Hanukkah" means to train up or dedicate, and the root work *hanak* means to make narrow. The idea of dedication involves limitation. If we are truly dedicated to the Lord, then by His Spirit we focus ourselves and limit our actions. As Judah Maccabee came to remove the enemy's defiling hold over God's Temple, so Yeshua came that we would be "delivered from the domain of darkness into the kingdom of His [God's] beloved Son" (Colossians 1:13).

As His temple, we recognize from Hanukkah that unless we are dedicated, we are not spiritually useful to God, and therefore we live unfulfilled lives. As we look at Yeshua's dedicated life we can understand how God works in our lives as He conforms us to the image of Messiah (Romans 8:29). Our dedication is seen in three ways: as a sanctuary, a son, and a servant.

THE BELIEVER AS A DEDICATED SANCTUARY

In 1 Kings 8:62-66 we see that the purpose of dedication was to bring spiritual intimacy and worship.

> Solomon offered for the sacrifice of peace offerings, which he offered to the LORD, 22,000 oxen and 120,000 sheep." (1 Kings 8:63)

This passage shows us that spiritual intimacy with God has its price. Imagine what this looked and sounded like at Solomon's temple. How much would 142,000 head of livestock have cost? Dedication is costly.

Think of what it cost the Maccabees to fight the mighty Syrian army for three years. Many lives were sacrificed for the cause of liberating and rededicating the Temple. In a similar way, Messiah gave His life as a sacrifice to redeem us as the Temple of God. Dedication is measured by sacrifice.

The Maccabees, Moses, and Solomon understood that God's dwelling place was dedicated to the Lord. In the same way, spiritual intimacy with God requires us to yield ourselves for God's use only.

> So the king and all the sons of Israel dedicated the house of the LORD. (1 Kings 8:63)

When the Temple was dedicated, it fulfilled God's purpose. When you are dedicated to Him, you find God's purpose for you as well. Your heart is His dwelling place, an altar for prayer. This is where we meet with God intimately. If you restrict your life "for God's use only," then you will find fulfillment.

At Hanukkah the Temple was rededicated, not for a once-a-week visit, but for daily service. For example, the priests did not announce, "Las Vegas night on Tuesdays, poker on Thursdays, and holy worship on the Sabbath." No, the priests understood that ten percent dedication meant a hundred percent desecration. As the temple of the Holy Spirit, are you desecrated or dedicated? Desecration is often found in vain religious activity, but genuine worship is found in sincere dedication. Is He in control of your life and your actions? Only cleansed and consecrated worship brings fulfillment in the Lord.

THE BELIEVER AS A DEDICATED SON

For all of us, spiritual maturity is the result of consistent dedication. Regarding this Solomon wrote:

> Train up a child in the way he should go: and when he
> is old, he will not depart from it. (Proverbs 22:6)

Here we see the process of dedication, which is based on a relationship. Even as a child is trained up in "the way he should go," spiritual maturity in God is achieved through a process of dedication. The Hebrew word translated "train up" is derived from the same word for Hanukkah. Children are to be trained in the truth.

Dedication is not just a matter of a well-rounded education, but rather being properly focused on the truth. For all of us, the lack of spiritual maturity comes from a lack of consistent dedication. Godly discipline in childhood brings godly self-discipline in adulthood.

To dedicate a child is to train up the child in light of who he actually is, just as God does with you. But remember, when we train up a child it is the dedication of the parents, not the child, that is being considered. More than just praying, reading the Bible, and hearing godly teaching, dedication is the consistent application of truth in a person's life.

With this is the promise: "...when he is old he will not depart from it." He may detour, but he will not depart. Some may ask, "What if you do all you can and your children still do not turn out as you had hoped?" Remember the story of the prodigal son? (Luke 15). In that parable the father represents God. He had two sons: one was self-righteous, and the other was an utterly wasteful person. If that father represents God, and both of His sons are moral failures, does that make God a failure? Of course not. Then what's the point? Even for God the job is not to produce perfect children, but to love imperfect children perfectly. Eventually the prodigal son returned home, for after all, he was still a son.

THE BELIEVER AS A DEDICATED SERVANT

In Genesis 14:13-16 we see the product of dedication, which is discipleship. This gives us insight into realizing spiritual victory in God.

> When Abram heard that his relative had been taken captive, he led out his *trained* men, born in his house, three hundred and eighteen, and went in pursuit as far as Dan. (Genesis 14:14)

There is that word again. Abraham's men were "trained" or "dedicated ones" (in Hebrew - *hanikim*). Those who were dedicated to their master's victory shared in the victory, for the Scripture says about them in verse 16:

> He brought back all the goods, and also brought back his relative Lot with his possessions, and also the women and the people.

What does dedication do for you as a servant of God? Those who completely give themselves to God will share in His glory. In the Scripture portion, those who were dedicated were led out to victory.

However, the undedicated did not share in the victory. Who does God use to free those dominated and ensnared by the enemy? He uses only the dedicated servants (*hanikim*). It is not our ability, but our availability that counts. The dedicated are spiritually successful, and

Messiah is the perfect example of a dedicated life. He is the true Servant of God:

> Just as the Son of Man did not come to be served, but to serve, and to give His life a ransom for many. (Matthew 20:28)

He came only to serve. He gave up the glory of heaven to become a servant (*shamash*) and fulfill the will of God, His Father. He is given us an example of true dedicated service.

> Yeshua answered, "Truly, truly, I say to you, the Son can do nothing of Himself, unless it is something He sees the Father doing; for whatever the Father does, these things the Son also does in like manner." (John. 5:19)

Yeshua is the servant, but also the true Son of God; the reality of God made manifest. He models for us the true sonship that faith brings. Finally, He is the true Sanctuary of God: "I saw no temple in it, for the Lord God the Almighty and the Lamb are its temple" (Revelation 21:22).

This minor winter holiday of Hanukkah, so often seen as a side-show to Christmas, is meant to focus our attention on an important question: who would the true Messiah of Israel be? Would he be a mere political deliverer, or something much more? In this season, let us dedicate ourselves to the service of the Divine King.

QUESTIONS FOR HANUKKAH:

1. What does "Hanukkah" mean and where is it found in the Scriptures?

2. What sorts of things did Antiochus do to the Jewish people and to the land of Israel?

3. Why would Messiah have celebrated Hanukkah? How did He do so?

4. When asked if He was the Messiah why didn't Yeshua just tell them directly who He is?

5. How do Yeshua's words and works testify that He is the Promised Messiah?

GOD IS GIVING DELIVERANCE

TO HIS PEOPLE

through

PURIM

CHAPTER 9

THE FEAST OF PURIM

פורים

GOD'S FAITHFULNESS TO ISRAEL

"They tried to kill us. We won. Let's eat!" This sort of works as a summary of most of our holidays. Well, at least it is true for Purim.

Every year on the fourteenth day of *Adar* (usually in March) Jewish people around the world celebrate Purim ("Lots"[1]). Traditions include the public reading or chanting of the entire Esther Scroll[2] and performing a Purim play (*Purimshpil*), which tells the Esther story. Though the story itself is dramatic, the plays can be quite comical and raucous. The audience participates by 'booing' and even rattling noise-makers at every mention of the villainous Haman while loudly cheering on Mordecai and Esther, the hero and heroine. Another tradition is baking and eating

---

[1] *Purim* means "lots," or the die cast to determine the date of the decree for the death of the Jews, Esther 9:24-26

[2] Called the *megillah*, or "scroll."

fruit filled triangle shaped pastry called *Hamantashen* in Yiddish and "Haman's ears" in Hebrew.

THE STORY OF ESTHER

Our story from the Book of Esther takes place in Shushan, the ancient capital city of Persia. It is here we are first introduced to King Ahasuerus[3], who ruled Persia 486-465 BCE. In the opening scene, the King is displeased with his queen, Vashti. This is because she would not display her beauty by wearing just a crown before the king's drunken friends. To save face, Ahasuerus decides to replace her with a more compliant, but no less beautiful candidate for queen.

Enter a Jewish girl named Haddassah, or in Babylonian, Esther. With a little help from her uncle Mordecai, Esther gets the job, and honestly more than she may have bargained for (Esther 2).

Mordecai not only counseled Esther into the position, but he worked as a guard for the king, where he providentially overheard and foiled a plan to assassinate the king (Esther 3). In the meantime the king unwittingly puts a vicious anti-Semite named Haman (boo!) into position as his Prime Minister. Filled with hatred, Haman decides to rid the empire of the Jews, especially Mordecai who would not bow down to him as was required in Shushan. Mordecai tells Esther to intercede with the king on behalf of her people. Though hesitant, after some coaxing and challenging, she goes to the king and exposes Haman's plot. Haman is hung on the gallows he had prepared for Mordecai, the Jews are saved, and Purim is established to remember this victorious event (Esther 9).

---

[3] "Ahasuerus" is the Hebrew name used throughout the book of Esther. It is a variant of Xerxes

That's the story, but questions remain: Why did Esther hesitate? Why was Haman doomed to fail (Esther 6:13)?

THE RESULT OF SPIRITUAL COMPROMISE

Esther is unique in the Bible in that the name of God is never mentioned. Why? Perhaps those who will not identify with God's call are not identified with God's name. These events take place fifty years after Cyrus permitted the Jewish people to leave Babylon and return to the Promised Land (2 Chronicles 36:22-23; Ezra 1:1-4). The book of Esther is written about those Jews that did not heed the call of God and return to the land of Israel.

God is faithful to His promises and will always providentially secure His people. But without a personal response, there is no testimony. Esther and Mordecai were among those who, out of convenience or preference decided to remain in Persia and not return to the land of Israel. Neglecting God's call leads to a downward spiritual spiral that we see in Esther's life. Consider her response to Mordecai when given the news of an official decree of her people's destruction; and that she is their apparent hope:

> All the king's servants and the people of the king's provinces know that for any man or woman who comes to the king to the inner court who is not summoned, he has but one law, that he be put to death, unless the king holds out to him the golden scepter so that he may live. And I have not been summoned to come to the king for these thirty days. (Esther 4:11)

With her people's existence threatened, why does Esther respond in such a self-serving manner? The point is not to merely sit in judgment: she is no worse than any of us! But she is one of us, and like any of us, Esther was concerned more for her own safety than the safety of her people.

Earlier, she was indifferent to Scriptural details. Since Esther was Jewish, she would have kept dietary restrictions according to the Law of Moses. However, the food that would have been provided in the King's palace was definitely not kosher. When she was provided with food she did not refuse (Esther 2:9).

She stands in contrast to Daniel, who in the Babylonian captivity, was faced with a similar situation. Daniel remained faithful and refused to eat food that would have been sacrificed to idols (Daniel 1:8). For Daniel, eating food offered to idols was the first step of spiritual compromise. The first step to moral failure may seem small, even inconsequential, but it is not. So many can think, "it's just a little lie, a small lust, a minor offence—what difference will it make." Small hinges can open big doors to a life of moral failure.

IDENTIFIED WITH A SINFUL WORLD

Then, "Esther did not make known her people or her kindred" (Esther 2:10). Though Moses, to his financial and political loss, chose to identify "with the people of God" and the faithfulness of God, Esther thought otherwise (Hebrews 11:24-26). She accepted counsel to hide her identity as a Jew, and therefore, her identification with the God of Israel.

Using worldly reasoning, perhaps Esther thought, "Why raise these problems so early? I can always tell the truth after I have the job." But in so doing Esther only reinforced her own shame, guilt and unbelief. Even after being chosen Queen she still hid her identity (Esther 2:20). Her omission was not just the practical matter of getting the job: it was sin.

SELFISH AMBITION

To be chosen as a new queen the young women were interviewed with the king at night. "In the evening she [Esther] would go in and in the morning she would return to the second harem" (Esther 2:12).

If you ever go to a job interview, where they tell you to visit the boss "in the evening and leave in the morning"– don't take that job! Believers are to "flee immorality"– do not submit to it for any reason (1 Corinthians 6:18). We have the example of Joseph who refused fornication as a means to advance his career, but Esther submitted to the immoral protocol of the day (Genesis 39:8). God is able to secure our lives by His grace as we depend upon and live for Him.

Esther won the beauty contest and "was taken to King Ahasuerus and was made queen instead of Vashti" (Esther 2:17). Esther considered it the opportunity of a lifetime to wed the pagan king. By this time Esther had no commitment to a godly life or any concern for a testimony for the Lord. To be "unequally yoked" with a non-believer is not merely to sin in the present, but to commit yourself to a lack of testimony in the future as well (2 Corinthians 6:14). During these five silent years, one can only imagine the many occasions for idolatry that Esther submitted herself to for the sake of her Queenly career.

He brought her to his royal palace in the tenth month in the seventh year of his reign... the first month in the twelfth year. (Esther 2:16; 3:7)

Esther accepted idol worship as a part of the state functions since it came with the job. In contrast, Shadrach, Meshach and Abednego went to the fires before submitting to idol worship (Daniel 3:17-18).

ESTHER'S SPIRITUAL CHALLENGE

God can use anyone, and in this case brought problems to break up Esther's self-centered life. God permitted a Haman, a vicious anti-Semite to shake up Esther's world. Though Mordecai exhorted her to intercede with the king on behalf of her people, Esther wanted no part of any plan that would endanger her.

It was risky to go uninvited into the king's presence. The ancient Greek historian Herodotus confirms this Persian custom that anyone who approached the king uninvited would be put to death– unless pardoned by the king.[4] Mordecai had one last challenge to the Queen.

> Do not imagine that you in the king's palace can escape any more than all the Jews. For if you remain silent at this time, relief and deliverance will arise for the Jews from another place and you and your father's house will perish. And who knows whether you have not attained royalty for such a time as this? (Esther 4:13-14)

As a result of Mordecai's exhortation, Esther repented, pleaded to the King on behalf of her people's welfare and the Jewish people were then preserved from extinction once again (Esther 4:15-16; 7:3-6; 9:20-25). What made such a change in Esther that she would risk it all to help her people? The truth of Mordecai's challenge encouraged Esther's timid heart.

---

[4] Herodotus, The Histories 3.118; Esther 4:11

First, he challenged the false security of her perception: "Do not imagine that you in the king's palace can escape any more than all the Jews." Esther could not live in a fantasy world where her cowardice would provide a means of escape. The foolish find their sense of satisfaction, significance and even their feeling of security in their vain imagination (Proverbs 18:11). This vanity of the mind assumes our disobedience to God will actually be our protection. People believe that their lies will protect– even promote them. However, we cannot insulate ourselves from God.

The vanity of our imagination is a result of our self-oriented unbelief (Romans 1:21). Yes, there is a way that seems right to a man, but the end of this "stinking thinking" is death.

> For the mind set on the flesh is death, but the mind set on the Spirit is life and peace, because the mind set on the flesh is hostile toward God; for it does not subject itself to the law of God, for it is not even able to do so. (Romans 8:6-7)

Therefore, we need to remove this vanity as a basis for security, and in trusting obedience yield our minds to Messiah Yeshua:

> For the weapons of our warfare are not carnal but mighty in God for pulling down strongholds, we are destroying speculations and every lofty thing raised up against the knowledge of God, and we are taking every thought captive to the obedience of Messiah. (2 Corinthians 10:4-5)

Mordecai then challenged the false security of Esther's passivity: "If you remain silent at this time, deliverance will arise for the Jews from another place and you and your father's house will perish."

Many people think that not doing evil is equal to doing righteousness. In Luke 16, the rich man did not actually do anything to hurt Lazarus. Still he found out too late that by not pro-actively helping this homeless man in his close circle, he was still guilty (Luke 16:19-25). The sin of omission—not doing what we should do—is as wicked to God as the sin of commission—doing what is wrong.

Esther must not be silent when her words could be the means of deliverance from destruction for the Jewish people. So also, believers today dare not think that they can keep silent about the Gospel when they know that it is the only means of saving the Jewish people and all people from judgment. Silence in this case would be a sin of omission. Scripture consistently encourages us to warn others of the judgment to come and the need to repent and believe.

> Son of man, I have appointed you a watchman to the house of Israel; whenever you hear a word from My mouth, warn them from Me. (Ezekiel: 3:17-21)

> Therefore everyone who confesses Me before men, I will also confess him before My Father who is in heaven. But whoever denies Me before men, I will also deny him before My Father who is in heaven. (Matthew 10:32-33)

> He said to them, "Thus it is written, that the Messiah would suffer and rise again from the dead the third day, and that repentance for forgiveness of sins would be

proclaimed in His name to all the nations, beginning from Jerusalem. You are witnesses of these things." (Luke 24:46-48).

You will receive power when the Holy Spirit has come upon you; and you shall be My witnesses both in Jerusalem, and in all Judea and Samaria, and even to the remotest part of the earth. (Acts 1:8)

Scripture clearly teaches believers to share the Good News with all people, yes, even to the Jew first. Even if in our disobedience we keep silent, God will be faithful to His word, "help will come from another place" and the Jewish people will live despite the Hamans, the Hitlers, and the Bin Ladens (Genesis 12:3; Jeremiah 31:35-37). Perhaps God would have raised up another country to destroy Persia, as He raised up the Medo-Persian Empire to destroy Israel's previous oppressor, Babylon (Daniel 5:30,31). Then Esther and her family would have died with the Persian royal household where she thought she was so secure. She could either identify with God, His promises and His people, or identify with His enemies.

MORDECAI'S PURIM CHALLENGE

Finally, Mordecai challenged the false security of Esther's position: "Who knows whether you have not attained royalty for such a time as this?" Esther had married Ahasuerus, the most powerful man of his time. Did she think that this marriage and queenly position would provide her with the security her soul needed? Sometimes people marry to fulfill their lives only to find that they are still just as lonely and empty. Neither marriage, nor career, nor wealth can fulfill a life. It is not the palace, but the promises of God which can satisfy our desires. As the Scripture states, "My God shall supply all your needs through His riches and glory in Messiah Yeshua" (Philippians 4:19), and "We are more than conquerors through Him who loved us" (Romans 8:37).

Our jobs, status in life, wealth and connections are not our security, but mere opportunities to share the Messiah. Our only true security is in our saving relationship with God. Let us not live as if we believe otherwise. Esther's position as Queen was not her security, but the opportunity providentially given by God.

The most secure place is not within the walls of a palace, but in the will of God. Esther's problem was imagining the fantasy of a spiritual middle ground, but there is no middle ground with God. Praise the Lord that Esther finally repents– "I will go into the king" (Esther 4:16). God brought a disobedient woman to repentance in order to save His people and demonstrate His faithfulness.

God had to shake up Esther's life and remove her vain defense system. This would bring Esther to where she could serve God and truly be secure in Him. A boy and his father were walking by the shore and saw workman knocking away the wooden props from the pier being built. "Dad why are they knocking down the wooden props?" asked the son. "So that the pier will rest more securely on the stone pilings," answered the father. Is God knocking away some of the "props" you have been using for false security in your life? He wants you to depend upon the foundation, which is the solid Rock of Messiah. God removes the false security of the flesh to replace it with the full security of faith.

Traditionally, Esther is seen as a true hero for saving her people from extinction. What then is the message of the Book of Esther? Simply this: God is faithful to keep His people and will use any ordinary person, if we will repent, trust and serve Him. God wants to use you today just as He used Esther long ago. Perhaps Mordecai's Purim challenge to Esther is God's challenge to you as well. Be spiritually pro-active in life– in your family, community and congregation. Do not keep silent; rather, share God's love in Yeshua with others.

THE ROOTS OF EVIL

One could only wonder what Haman must have been thinking? That is, until you realize that the background of these two foes, Mordecai and Haman, gives further insight into their rivalry. In Esther 2:5 we read of Mordecai: "A Jew whose name was Mordecai, the son of Jair, the son of Shimei, the son of Kish, a Benjamite."

To the careful student of the Scriptures, the name son of Kish reminds us of King Saul an ancestor of Mordecai (1 Samuel 9:1-3). We read in Esther 3:1 of Haman's ancestry, "Haman, the son of Hammedatha the Agagite." According to Scripture and Jewish tradition this family name "Agagite" comes from the Amalekite king, Agag, who was an enemy of Israel during King Saul's reign (1 Samuel 15:7-33). The book of Esther subtly informs us that Haman, a descendant of Agag, and Mordecai, a descendant of Saul, have inherited the ancient feud between the Amalekites and the Israelites.

There are certain spiritual principles at work in this scenario. The Scriptures state that King Saul was commanded to destroy the entire anti-Semitic tribe of the

Amalekites (1 Samuel 15:1-3; Exodus 17:8-16). Though Saul conquered the Amalekites in battle, he kept back some of the best of the spoil for a so called sacrifice, along with their king Agag as a personal trophy. The next day the prophet Samuel rebuked Saul for his disobedience, then slew Agag himself (1 Samuel 15:33). But Agag lived that one night and it was long enough to pass along his seed and perpetuate the Amalekites and their anti-Jewish hostilities, in the person of Haman. In our own lives as well, allowing sin to live just one more day, can prove to be deadly: one more day is one day too many.

There is a parallel spiritual principle in Mordecai's own providential ancestry. This ancestor Shimei of Kish and Saul's family were well known to David.

During David's flight from his son Absalom's attempted coup, Shimei had cursed David (2 Samuel 16:5). But upon David's return to Jerusalem and to the throne, he pardoned Shimei and allowed him to live. This showed amazing patience for David, who was much better known for his severe reactions to such slights. David perceived that the Lord was involved in this matter (2 Samuel 16:11-12).

In later years when David was upon death's door, he ordered his son Solomon to put Shimei to death after Shimei was old and would have already had his children (1 Kings 2:8,36-46). In God's providence, He allowed Saul's vanity to permit Agag to live another day. In David's case, God restrained David's passions which allowed Mordecai to counter the effects of Haman. All of this demonstrates God's promises to preserve His people by His grace, while He awakens them from their unbelief.

WHY HAMAN MUST FAIL

Though Agag's future seed Haman had meant to do evil, God had also providentially prepared a Shimei for good through his future seed Mordecai. God in His mercy graciously allowed Saul's own weakness with Agag to be countered through Saul's own seed in Mordecai. So in the providence of God, even Saul would prove that through man's weakness God's grace is truly sufficient for our lives. We can trust God to overrule our weaknesses, and be confident that His grace will show itself sufficient. Our boast is always in the Lord.

Therefore, Mordecai refused to humble himself to Haman. First of all, it would be considered idolatry, since only God should have our worshipful prostration. Secondly, Mordecai refused to yield to the traditional enemy of Israel; no self-respecting son of Benjamin would bow before the ancient Amalekite descendant, an enemy of the Jewish people. Consequently, Haman was humiliated and wanted to kill Mordecai, and all of Mordecai's people. He even built a gallows seventy-five feet high to hang Mordecai on. But after a ironic turn of events, Haman found himself being commanded by the king to honor, Mordecai. He brought this news to his wife and cronies.

> Haman recounted to Zeresh his wife and all his friends everything that had happened to him. Then his wise men and Zeresh his wife said to him, "If Mordecai, before whom you have begun to fall, is of Jewish origin (*mizera' yehudim*), you will not overcome him, but will surely fall before him." (Esther 6:13)

The Hebrew is emphatic: "falling you will fall before him! (*nafol tipol lifanav*)." Haman's ruin was sure; he could not stand against Mordecai the Jew. And yet, those who now saw the handwriting on the wall were the same people who had earlier advised Haman to hang Mordecai (Esther 5:14). How did Haman's advisers know of his certain failure? They had been taught historically, Biblically, and prophetically.

Historically: In the history of the last 50 years, Haman's advisers had seen how God miraculously worked through Cyrus their King. Though Babylon and Persia had exiled the Jewish people for 70 years from their homeland, King Cyrus's decree released them to return, even as was prophesied (Jeremiah 29:10).

Biblically: While the Jewish people were in Babylon, which was eventually absorbed into Persia, the Babylonians had the writings of the prophet Daniel in their possession. In the Book of Daniel the uniqueness, power and purpose of the God of Israel was revealed to this kingdom:

> Then King Nebuchadnezzar fell on his face and did homage to Daniel. The king answered Daniel and said, "Surely your God is a God of gods and a Lord of kings and a revealer of mysteries, since you have been able to reveal this mystery." (Daniel 2:46-47)

> "He delivers and rescues and performs signs and wonders in heaven and on earth, who has also delivered Daniel from the power of the lions." (Daniel 6:27)

> "Then the sovereignty, the dominion and the greatness of all the kingdoms under the whole heaven will be given to the people of the saints of the Highest One." (Daniel 7:27)

Prophetically: Earlier, a wise man from that region, Balaam, had tried his hand at this "cursing Israel" business, and had found it to be a bad idea.

> How shall I curse whom God has not cursed? And how can I denounce whom the LORD has not denounced? Blessed is everyone who blesses you (Israel), and cursed is everyone who curses you. I see him, but not now; I behold him, but not near; a star shall come forth from Jacob, a scepter shall rise from Israel, One from Jacob shall have dominion. (Numbers 23:8,20,23; 24:9,17,19)

It was from this same area that the Magi would come at the time of Messiah's birth (Matthew 2:1-8). The Magi recognized the truth of Balaam's words, that the Jews were the hope of the world, since through them and them alone, the Messiah would come (Genesis 22:18).

Therefore because of the historical, Biblical and prophetic truth, Haman's advisors knew that he was doomed to fail. For as Balaam said, "Blessed is everyone who blesses you, and cursed is everyone who curses you" (Numbers 24:9). This was first declared by God Himself to Abraham:

> I will make you a great nation, and I will bless you and I will make your name great; and so you will be a blessing; and I will bless those who bless you, and the one who curses you I will curse. And in you all the families of the earth will be blessed. (Genesis 12:2-3)

Notice the text: those who bless is plural, those who curse is singular. The desire of God is to bless many and curse few. When you do not bless the Jewish people you must ultimately fail, for you are contrary to God's desire and nature, which is love (1 John 4:8,16).

We are created in the image of God, and we are to be an instrument of blessing, not cursing; of love, not hate. Haman was wrong and ultimately had to fail. The Nazis, the jihadists and all racists are wrong and ultimately will fail. If you hate Jewish people you are wrong, and you will ultimately fail. To bless Abraham is to bless the God of Abraham through faith and obedience.

IDENTIFYING WITH GOD'S CALL

Identifying with the God's calling has always been evidenced by identifying with the God's people. Notice how Moses identified with the call of God on his life.

> By faith Moses, when he had grown up, refused to be called the son of Pharaoh's daughter, choosing rather to endure ill-treatment with the people of God than to enjoy the passing pleasures of sin, considering the reproach of Messiah greater riches than the treasures of Egypt; for he was looking to the reward. (Hebrews 11:24-26)

Daniel chose to break the law of man, rather than break faith with God. Though a captive in Babylon, he identified with his people and homeland.

> Now when Daniel knew that the document was signed, he entered his house (now in his roof chamber he had windows open toward Jerusalem); and he continued kneeling on his knees three times a day, praying and giving thanks before his God, as he had been doing previously. (Daniel 6:10)

Ruth though not Jewish herself, identified with the Jewish people because she first identified with God.

> Ruth said, "Do not urge me to leave you or turn back from following you; for where you go, I will go, and where you lodge, I will lodge. Your people shall be my people, and your God, my God." (Ruth 1:16)

Even though Paul was called to minister to the Gentiles, he lived as a Jew and identified himself with his people throughout his ministry.

> But Paul said, "I am a Jew of Tarsus in Cilicia, ... I am a Jew, born in Tarsus of Cilicia." "I say then, God has not rejected His people has He? May it never be! For I too am an Israelite, a descendant of Abraham, of the tribe of Benjamin. God will not forsake a people who He foreknew." (Acts 21:39; 22:3; Romans 11:1-2)

What was Paul's motivation? He was convinced that God is faithful and His promises are unchanging. Paul's commitment was demonstrated through his influence on other Jewish believers like Timothy.

> Paul came also to Derbe and to Lystra. And a disciple was there, named Timothy, the son of a Jewish woman who was a believer, but his father was a Greek, and he was well spoken of by the brethren who were in Lystra and Iconium. Paul wanted this man to go with him; and he took him and circumcised him because of the Jews who were in those parts, for they all knew that his father was a Greek. (Acts 16:1-3)

Why did Paul circumcise Timothy? Because circumcision identifies the Jewish male with the physical descent of the Abrahamic Covenant (Genesis 17:10). For Jewish believers, the *bris*[5] is still an ongoing testimony of God's faithfulness to Israel.

Timothy is identified as a Jew through circumcision. What difference would this make? The "Jews in those parts" would have no basis to think that faith in Yeshua denies the promises made to Israel; rather, it testifies that Yeshua is the fulfillment of those promises. Whether it was Moses, Daniel, Joseph, Ruth, Paul or Timothy, or you, the challenge of faith is always this: Do we believe that God is faithful to His promises? Will we be willing to identify with Him and His people?

Esther's failure to identify with God's purpose and people was symptomatic of the problem for all who stayed behind in Babylon. God cared for His people, and therefore confronted the problem head-on by allowing a Haman to arise and force the issue.

WHY A CHOSEN PEOPLE?

Throughout history the Jewish people have suffered persecution like no other ethnic group. Being the chosen people of God has caused us to endure the wrath of the adversary, Satan. That which God loves, Satan hates. However, the enduring existence of the Jewish people is undeniable evidence of the existence of God, and a testimony to His sovereignty, His omnipotence, and His ultimate plan for Israel and all mankind:

> Thus says the LORD, Who gives the sun for a light by day, The ordinances of the moon and the stars for a

---

[5] "covenant"; circumcision ceremony, also called *brit milah*

light by night, Who disturbs the sea, And its waves roar (The LORD of hosts is His name): If those ordinances depart from before Me, says the LORD, then the seed of Israel shall also cease from being a nation before Me forever. (Jeremiah 31:35-36)

In this passage the Lord says that if you want to completely destroy the Jewish people (and some do), all you have to do is reach up in the sky and pull down the sun, moon and the stars from their established positions and orbits in the universe. However, it is not going to happen, though many have tried. The Pharaohs, Hamans, and Hitlers of history would have done well to read and heed the word of God, as would many anti-Semites in our day. Despite them all, the word of our God endures forever (Isaiah 40:8; 1 Peter 1:24-25).

God desired a people He could reveal Himself to and through them He would reveal Himself to all mankind. The fact that God chose the Jewish people is confirmed through the Scripture and history. "Why did God choose the Jews?" Was it because we are a righteous people? No. In fact God says in Deuteronomy 9:6 that we are a "stubborn people." Is it because we had the most potential? Not really. The opposite seems to be implied in the very Scripture that answers the question. In Deuteronomy 7:6-8, God speaks through Moses to Israel, saying:

The LORD your God has chosen you to be a people for Himself ...The LORD did not set His love on you nor choose you because you were more in number than any other people, for you were the least of all peoples; but because the LORD loves you.

God's choice was born out of love; and He loves us because He loves us. It is about Him, not us. God chose the "least" of all peoples in order to demonstrate that His sovereign love, grace and promises can keep even the weakest of all people.

In this way all people, no matter how weak they may be can find hope and help in the eternal love of God. In the New Covenant this same principle is applied.

> For consider your calling, brethren, that there were not many wise according to the flesh, not many mighty, not many noble; but God has chosen the foolish things of the world to shame the wise, and God has chosen the weak things of the world to shame the things which are strong, and the base things of the world and the despised, God has chosen, the things that are not, that He might nullify the things that are, that no man should boast before God. (1 Corinthians 1:26-29)

Through Israel God revealed His Word, His plan, and ultimately the Messiah, the Savior of the world. Though the nation of Israel rejected her Messiah, God remains faithful to His people. There is a remnant according to grace. At Messiah's first coming, according to Dr. Louis Goldberg, former Professor of Jewish Studies at *Moody Bible Institute,* it is estimated that up to one fourth of Israel's population came to faith in Yeshua as the Messiah in the first century.[6] Even today Jewish people from every nation including Israel are coming to faith in Yeshua. Israel remains the centerpiece of the plan of God, and will be until Messiah comes again to establish His reign from

---

6 From the keynote message that Dr. Goldberg shared at a Fellowship of Messianic Congregations' conference in the early 1990's

Jerusalem. In light of all this, Satan is trying to destroy the Jewish people, and is intensifying his efforts as the end of this age draws to its close.

Gentile believers in Yeshua need to identify with the Jewish people. Notice what it says in Esther 9:27, "The Jews established and imposed it upon themselves and their descendants and all who would join them, that without fail they should celebrate ... every year."

Gentile believers can "join with" the Jewish people by standing against anti-Semitism, pro-actively sharing the Good News, praying for the Peace of Jerusalem and identifying with the remnant of Israel, who are Jewish believers in Yeshua. This is one reason why so many believing Gentiles are attending Messianic congregations: they identify with God's unfailing promises. It is crucial for Jewish believers to identify themselves as Jews.

If we, as Jewish believers, raise our children in a culturally Gentile expression of faith, are we not subtly saying to our children, "Don't tell them you're a Jew!" We should raise our children in such a way that they will grow spiritually and testify powerfully *Am Yisrael Chai B'Yeshua HaMashiach*, "the people of Israel live in Yeshua the Messiah!" It is only when Jewish believers identify themselves as Jews, that they identify with God's unchanging call and purpose regarding Israel.

SATAN'S ANTI-SEMITIC STRATEGY

When Messiah returns to earth at His second coming He will imprison Satan for 1000 years (1 Peter 5:8, Revelation 20:1-3). Since Messiah's second coming is contingent on Israel's repentance as a nation, Satan knows that his time is short, and is doing everything he

can to prevent Jewish people from hearing the Good News (Revelation 12:12). This fact is reiterated by Peter in Acts 3:19-21:

> Therefore repent and return, so that your sins may be wiped away, in order that times of refreshing may come from the presence of the Lord; and that He may send Yeshua the Messiah appointed for you, whom heaven must receive until the period of restoration of all things about which God spoke by the mouth of His holy prophets from ancient time.

The return of the Lord depends upon the repentance of Israel. In order for Satan to prevent the return of Messiah, he must prevent the Jewish people from coming to faith in Yeshua: confessing Isaiah 53, thereby fulfilling Zechariah 12:10. There are basically two aspects to his dark strategy:

1. Stop Jews from living: Annihilation
2. Stop Jews from living as Jews: Assimilation

The fact that history is replete with rabid anti-Semitism and violence against the Jewish people can only be explained by the presence and plan of Satan. He utilized Hitlers and Hamans to pursue the annihilation of Jewish people. He has even produced so-called Christians as the perpetrators of anti-Semitic hatred, so much so that Yeshua seems to be the leader of the religion of our enemies. Is it any wonder that Jewish people find it so bizarre to consider, let alone confess Yeshua as Lord?

Satan's contingency plan to assimilate Jews seems more subtle, but actually is very effective. Keeping Jews from living as Jews is the most devious ploy of all. Even when a Jew comes to believe in Yeshua, Satan has attempted

to make living a Jewish lifestyle seem unnecessary, inconvenient, and even unbiblical.

Let us not passively play a part in Satan's plan to destroy the Jewish people, by teaching Jewish believers that they are no longer Jews, or should stop identifying themselves as Jews. As a result, you will hear the children of these same Jewish believers say things like, "I think my grandfather was Jewish." If you are a Jewish believer, do not let the Jewish testimony as a nation before God end with you, but instead say with the apostle Paul, "I am a Jew..." (Acts 22:3).

GOD LOVES EVERYBODY

It is not just that God has in His heart a soft spot for one people; He is concerned about all people, and through Abraham, God chose to bless all the families of the earth. God will ultimately use Israel again as His instrument of influence in the world, and He promises that Israel is the key to God's international blessing program. God states to Abraham, "and in your seed will all the nations of the earth be blessed" (Genesis 22:18). Notice it says, "in your seed" rather than seeds. Thus it was his seed: Isaac, not Ishmael, Jacob, rather than Esau, and then his seed through Judah, David, and finally to Yeshua. As the New Covenant teaches:

> The promises were spoken to Abraham and to his seed. The Scripture does not say 'and to seeds,' meaning many people, but 'and to your seed,' meaning one person, who is Messiah. (Galatians 3:16)

> He redeemed us in order that the blessing of Abraham might come to the Gentiles through Messiah Yeshua. (Galatians 3:14)

As "God so loved the world," therefore all Hamans have to fail. And they will fail. It has been said, when God loves, He loves a world, and when He gives, He gives His Son. There is an ultimate victory for all people, for all who will believe in Yeshua the Messiah, the ultimate seed of Abraham. God could not let the Jewish people be destroyed for through the line of David Messiah came and will return again. Therefore, let us live in view of His return to be an instrument of blessing to Jewish people, and to all people.

QUESTIONS FOR PURIM:

1. Why did God choose the Jewish people?

2. Who are the main characters in the book of Esther?

3. What are some of the ways that Esther was spiritually compromised?

4. How is God's providence evident in the ancestry of Mordecai and Haman?

5. What is Satan's anti-Semitic program?

6. How do we know this plan will fail?

7. What does this book mean for the Jewish people and all people today?

EPILOGUE

SHOULD WE KEEP THE FEASTS TODAY?

A few years ago I was encouraged to see young people wearing WWJD wristbands. I was delighted to think that as these committed believers went through their day facing various issues, they would ask themselves, "What Would Jesus Do?" I prayed for them to have the courage to follow Messiah's example in those challenging moments.

Over time I saw fewer and fewer "WWJD" wristbands, and I figured another fad had come and gone. However the question raises a vital issue. In order to understand what Yeshua would do we need to examine how He lived. When we study the life of Yeshua from a Jewish frame of reference it becomes easier to understand just what was important to Him and what example He wanted us to follow. Scripture clearly teaches that Yeshua observed Hanukkah, the Feast of Tabernacles, and Passover. In fact, the reason that we know Yeshua ministered for just over three years is because John's Good News account records three Passovers Yeshua celebrated.

It seems we can often become distracted by man-made ideas that relate to various celebrations and forget the beautiful truths that our faith is founded upon.

Yeshua, the Apostles, and all the first century believers understood Messiah's Resurrection in light of the prophetically central events of Passover and First Fruits. With the ultimate focus of our redemption being the Lamb of God, Passover helps us understand the meaning of redemption, and the absolute necessity of having resurrection life in Yeshua. In fact, in order to continually appreciate the new life that we have in the Lord, Paul expected all believers to keep the feast of Passover. Thus, Passover redemption is the foundation of our First Fruits resurrection, our Pentecost experience, and our anticipation of the Feast of Trumpets, Day of Atonement, and the Feast of Tabernacles.

Yet, many believers are unaware of God's appointment calendar clearly given to us in Leviticus 23. Why do most believers in Yeshua no longer celebrate the feasts?

In order to understand why this took place we must be aware of the history of the church, so that it can be contrasted with what the Bible actually teaches. Now, we must recognize that historic church councils have helped to articulate and distinguish biblical truth from error on many crucial issues of the faith.

Unfortunately, in the fourth and fifth centuries, these same councils made questionable decisions pertaining specifically to Jewish people and the Jewish essence of our faith. Such decrees were made to separate the faith from its "Jewish roots." The Council of Nicea in AD 326 and

223

the Synod of Sardica in AD 344, influenced by several powerful and anti-Semitic church leaders conducted a deliberate and apparently quite successful effort to remove all Jewish expressions of the faith from the celebration of the faith.

There were various reasons these decrees were developed. In some cases it was to demonstrate the superiority of Christianity over Judaism, and of the church over the synagogue. Also, Emperor Constantine insisted on unity in his Roman Empire, and that meant religious unity as well through his new state religion, Christianity.[1] This unity meant defining the enemy:

> When the question relative to the sacred festival of Easter arose, it was universally thought ... to be particularly unworthy for this, the holiest of all festivals, to follow the custom of the Jews, who had soiled their hands with the most fearful of crimes, and whose minds were blinded. In rejecting their custom, we may transmit to our descendants the legitimate mode of celebrating Easter... We ought not, therefore, to have anything in common with the Jews, for the Saviour has shown us another way... we desire, dearest brethren, to separate ourselves from the detestable company of the Jews... How can they be in the right, they who, after the death of the Saviour, have no longer been led by reason but by wild violence, as their delusion may urge them? They do not possess the truth in this Easter question... it would still be your duty not to tarnish your soul by communications with such wicked people [the Jews]... For this reason, a Divine Providence wills... on the one hand, it is our duty not to have anything in common with the murderers of our Lord; and as, on

1 *The Church and The Jews*, Dan Gruber, Elijah Publishing, 2001, 37.

the other, the custom now followed by the Churches of the West, of the South, and of the North, and by some of those of the East... that we should have nothing in common with the Jews.[2]

What was intended to be some sort of victory for the church has instead meant confusion for many believers. The student tries without success to relate the teaching of Scripture to the replacement traditions which have been handed down through history.

Worse, these anti-Jewish decrees were devastating to the Gentile believer's witness to the Jewish community. When Gentile believers are unaware of the Jewish essence of their faith, when Yeshua's death and resurrection is removed from its Jewish context, then the fulfillment of the Messianic hope, which is found only in Yeshua, is all but hidden from the Jewish community.

The blatant removal of the Jewish roots of Scripture, accomplishing devastating results for the body of believers today, is really a symptom of a deeper problem of the heart. The calling of Gentile believers has always been to make the Jewish people jealous of faith in Yeshua, the Jewish Messiah (Romans 11:11, 17). But rejection of the Jewish people and their "customs" has turned this glorious calling on its head, making it seem an absurd, even malicious joke. Consider how much time, effort and money believers put into celebrating Christmas and Easter, and how little time is given to the Feasts of the Lord. To separate Jewishness from the Good News effectively estranges this message from the Jewish people. The story of Yeshua, forgiveness of sins, and being made right before God is presented out of context.

---

2 from the Letter of the Emperor to all those not present at the Council, as found in Eusebius, Vita Cont., Lib.iii., 18-20

What can be done? There is hope! We have a rich heritage and history of faith waiting to be discovered in the Scriptures. And celebrations are not meant to merely be read and about studied, but celebrated! One step to reclaim what God has for you in Messiah is to encourage your congregation to enjoy an annual Passover Seder which can then lead to a celebration of Messiah's resurrection. Some of the recommended resources give practical suggestions for observing the other days. Let us go past mere traditions and follow the truth, looking unto Yeshua as the substance of our celebrations.

You can make a difference in your family, congregation and community. Who knows? Perhaps God has His hand on your life "for such a time as this!"

REDEMPTION IN

GOD'S WORK	FEAST	LEV. 23	MONTH
GAINING HIS PEOPLE	PASSOVER	v. 4-5	NISSAN 1ST MONTH
	UNLEAVENED BREAD	v. 6-8	NISSAN 1ST MONTH
	FIRSTFRUITS	v. 9-14	NISSAN 1ST MONTH
GROUNDING HIS PEOPLE	WEEKS OR PENTECOST	v. 15-21	SIVAN 3RD MONTH
	WORK IN THE FIELDS	v. 22	SUMMER MONTHS
GATHERING HIS PEOPLE	TRUMPETS OR NEW YEAR	v. 23-25	TISHREI 7TH MONTH
	DAY OF ATONEMENT	v. 26-32	TISHREI 7TH MONTH
	BOOTHS OR TABERNACLES	v. 33-44	TISHREI 7TH MONTH

THE FEASTS OF ISRAEL

MEANING	FULFILLMENT	GOD'S RESULT
RANSOM OF SOUL	1 COR. 5:7	SALVATION
REMOVAL OF SIN	1 COR. 5:8	
RESURRECTION OF SAVIOR	1 COR. 15:21-23	
REDEEMED BODY	JAMES 1:18 ACTS 2:1-10	SANCTIFICATION
REACHING AND REAPING	MATT. 28:18-20 ACTS 1:8	
RAPTURE OF HIS BODY	1 COR. 15:52 1 THES. 4:16, 17	GLORIFICATION
REGENERATION OF ISRAEL	ZECH. 12:10-13:1 MATT. 23:39	
REIGN OF MESSIAH	ZECH. 14:16 REV. 7:9, 15	

A Glossary of
Jewish and Messianic Terminology

AFIKOMEN– Literally, "That which comes after." Piece of matzah that is hidden during the SEDER, to be found and eaten at the third cup.

B.C.E.– "Before the Common Era," also referred to as "BC" (Before Christ).

BRIS– or *brit*, "covenant," the circumcision ceremony. Sign of the Abrahamic Covenant (Gen. 17:9-14).

BRIT CHADASHAH– "New Covenant," the Apostolic Writings, often called the "New Testament." The term is from Jeremiah 31:31.

C.E.– "Common Era" also referred to as "AD," Latin for *Anno Domini*, "in the Year of our Lord."

ECHAD– Hebrew for "one" or "unity"; *Echad* is used in the SHEMA "...the LORD is One" (Deut. 6:4).

FIRSTFRUITS– first portion of the harvest, can refer to either REISHIT (chapter 3) or SHAVUOT (chapter 4).

HANUKKAH– "dedication," the feast commemorating the rebuilding and dedication of the Temple after its desecration by Syrian invaders (see chapter 8).

HANUKIYAH– the special *menorah* (lamp) used on the Feast of Dedication containing eight lights (for eight nights) plus one "servant candle" (SHAMASH).

HASHEM– "the Name," a reverent and traditional way of referring to God. It refers specifically to his four-letter personal name, rendered in many English Bibles as "LORD," and called the "tetragrammaton" (י *yud*, ה *hey*, ו *vav*, ה *hey*; note: Hebrew is written right to left).

KETUVIM– "Writings," the third section of the Hebrew Bible (after the TORAH and NEVI'IM), whose books include Psalms, Proverbs, Job, Song of Songs, and more.

LULAV– combination of willow, myrtle, and palm branches waved on SUKKOT.

MATZAH– "unleavened bread," bread made without yeast.

MESSIAH– Heb. *Mashiach*, literally, "Anointed One" as a prince, or King of Israel; the Greek equivalent of this word is *christos*, which transliterated into English, is "Christ."

MIKVEH– "standing, collected water," used for ceremonial washing, also known as TEVILAH from "to dip, plunge." Both words are used for immersion or "baptism."

NEVI'IM– "Prophets," the second section of the TENAKH.

OLAM HAZEH– "this present age."

OLAM HABA– "the world to come."

OMER– "sheaf," the bundle of barley used in the Firstfruits offering, after the Temple came to be identified with *sefirat ha'omer* ("the counting of the omer"), the counting of days from FIRSTFRUITS to Pentecost or SHAVUOT.

PASSOVER– Heb. *Pesach,* a holiday commemorating the rescue of the children of Israel from Egypt, and pointing to the sacrificial death of Messiah (see chapter 2).

PURIM– "lots," the holiday based on the story of Esther (see chapter 9).

REISHIT– Lit. "beginning," Biblical word used for FIRSTFRUITS (Lev. 23:10, ray-*sheet,* see chapter 3)

RUACH HAKODESH– "the Holy Spirit."

ROSH HASHANAH– "the head of the year," traditional Jewish New Year stemming from the Feast of Trumpets in Leviticus 23. See also YOM TERUAH (see chapter 5).

SEDER– "order," referring to the order of the Passover meal (see chapter 2).

SEPTUAGINT– "Seventy." Greek translation of the Tanakh by 70 rabbis, approximately 180 BC.

SHAMASH– "servant," or the servant candle used to light a HANUKIYAH.

SHAVUOT– "weeks"; in Greek, Pentecost; also called *Chag Ha-Bikkurim* or "the feast of Firstfruits" (see chapter 4, for barley harvest, see REISHIT).

SHEMA– "hear," refers to the text of Deuteronomy 6:4

SUKKOT– Hebrew for "booths" or temporary shelter; Feast to remember God's provision and protection in the wilderness wanderings, celebrated by creating and living in makeshift dwellings for eight days (pronounced "sue-*coat*"; one "booth" is a *sukkah;* see chapter 7)

SYNAGOGUE– "assembly," an adopted Greek word for a house of prayer, study, and assembly.

TALMUD– "study," compiled from AD 200-500, a collection of commentary and rabbinic legal discourse. Made up of Mishnah and Gemara, there is both a Babylonian and Jerusalem Talmud, with the Babylonian Talmud being much larger and carrying more authority.

TENAKH– The Hebrew Scriptures, or "Old Testament." The word is an acronym whose consonants (T-N-K) stand for TORAH (the Five Books of Moses); NEVIIM (the Prophets); KETUVIM ("Writings").

TORAH– "Instruction," also used to refer to the first five books of Moses (the Pentateuch).

YAMIM NORAIM– "Days of Awe," the ten days between ROSH HASHANAH and YOM KIPPUR.

YESHUA– the Hebrew name of Messiah, often transliterated through the Greek as "Jesus," meaning "the Lord is salvation," or "the Lord saves."

YOM KIPPUR– "Day of Atonement," the close of the High Holy Days, considered the holiest day of the year in traditional Judaism (see chapter 6).

YOM TERUAH– "day of blowing," or the Feast of Trumpets, this day begins the High Holy Days, Fall Feasts, and is the traditional New Year (see chapter 5).

ZIKKARON– Heb. "remembrance" or "memorial," also refers to the practice of partaking "the Lord's Supper," eating bread and drinking the cup (based on the AFIKOMEN and third cup of a traditional SEDER).

BIBLIOGRAPHY

Bonar, Andrew, *A Commentary on the Book of Leviticus*, Grand Rapids, Baker Book House, 1978

Edersheim, Dr. Alfred, *The Temple: Its Ministry and Services as They Were at the Time of Jesus Christ*, London, The Religious Tract Society

Finkel, Avraham Yaakov, *The Essence of the Holy Days: Insights From the Jewish Sages*, Northvale, Jason Aronson, Inc., 1993

Glaser, Mitch and Zhava, *The Fall Feasts of Israel.* Chicago, Moody Press, 1987

Kasdan, Barney, *God's Appointed Times*, Messianic Jewish Publishers, 1993

Ritchie, John, *Feasts of Jehovah*, Grand Rapids, Kregel Publications, 1982

Rosen, Ceil and Moishe, *Christ in the Passover: Why is This Night Different?* Chicago, Moody Press, 1978

Rosenbaum, Rev. M. and Dr. A. M. Silbermann, *Pentateuch with Rashi's Commentary, Leviticus*, New York, Hebrew Publishing Company

Schauss, Hayyim, *Guide to Jewish Holy Days: History and Observance,* New York, Schocken Books, 1968

Seiss, Joseph A., *Gospel in Leviticus,* Grand Rapids, Kregel Publications, 1904

BOOKS AND MATERIALS BY
WORD OF MESSIAH MINISTRIES

Messianic Foundations: Fulfill Your Calling in the Jewish Messiah - offers a vision of the Messianic Movement motivated by the testimony that Yeshua is God's faithfulness to Israel.

Messianic Discipleship: Following Yeshua, Growing in Messiah - leads the reader through a Jewish discipleship course, dealing with the essentials of Messianic faith.

The Messianic Answer Book - answers to the 15 most asked questions Jewish people have about the faith. Excellent tool for sharing with those seeking answers.

Even You Can Share The Jewish Messiah - a short booklet with key information on sharing Yeshua with friends and neighbors, even "to the Jew first" (Romans 1:16).

The Messianic Passover Haggadah - the perfect guide for conducting your own Passover Seder.

Messianic Wisdom: Practical Scriptural Answers for Your Life - get a grasp on Messianic Jewish issues and living out your faith in Messiah. Essential and inspiring, this book is for every growing disciple of Yeshua.

Messianic Life Lessons from the Book of Ruth - an in-depth, information-rich devotional commentary on what is a priceless book of restoration from the Tanakh.

Messianic Life Lessons from the Book of Jonah - do you want to know God's will for your life? Jonah proves that this alone will not help! A slender commentary on this book about Israel's mission to the Gentiles.

For more information, please contact us at:

WORD OF MESSIAH MINISTRIES
P.O. BOX 79238
CHARLOTTE, NC
28271, USA

PHONE/FAX: (704) 544-1948

Visit our website at:

WWW.WORDOFMESSIAH.ORG